P9-CKA-030

THE HEIRS OF DONNE AND JONSON

THE HEIRS
OF
DONNE AND JONSON

⟨⟩∞∞∞◎◯◎∞∞⟨⟩

JOSEPH H. SUMMERS

1970

OXFORD UNIVERSITY PRESS

NEW YORK AND LONDON

FOR
HELEN GARDNER
&
DOUGLAS BUSH

CONTENTS

PREFACE

THE chapters in this book are rewritten versions of lectures I gave at Oxford during Hilary term of 1967. I took that opportunity to get down as concisely as possible my most persistent notions about reading English poetry of the earlier seventeenth century. My central ideas are simple and not at all novel: that most of the interesting poets of the period were in some sense heirs of both Donne and Jonson and that they wrote successfully a large number of different kinds of poetry. One of my underlying prejudiced convictions undoubtedly surfaces a number of times: that if one is chiefly interested in poetry rather than writing examinations or defending theses, one should probably spend as little time as possible defining 'a poem' or 'a Renaissance poem,' or even 'a metaphysical' or 'a seventeenth century poem' and as much as possible reading all the extant poetry—and prose —written by interesting individual poets. My conclusions are therefore predictably (and perhaps hopelessly) pluralistic: granted the general condition of the language, the literary and intellectual currents, the 'spirit of the age,' and other large and vaguely apprehended abstractions, for the seventeenth century as for other periods one can discover almost as many aesthetics as there are interesting poets. A reading of the seventeenth-century poets in particular suggests considerably more various (and I believe more interesting) notions of 'poetry,' 'the poem,' and perhaps 'the poet' than are generally current today.

I have tried to preserve a sense of the mixed audience for which the lectures were originally delivered (undergraduates, graduates, teachers, research scholars, casual visitors) in the hope for a similarly mixed group of readers.

I have therefore kept my annotations to a perhaps inde-
cent minimum. Since I do not believe the seventeenth-
century poets wrote primarily for scholars or antiquarians
or wished their texts to appear idiosyncratic or quaint, I
have quoted them in my own conservatively modernized
texts (based usually on the monumental Oxford English
Texts) in which I have tried to preserve as much as possible
of the original meanings and sounds (including significant
ambiguities) with the fewest possible distractions for a
modern reader.

My indebtednesses are manifold. Any scholarly reader
will know how much I owe to the mass of modern criticism and scholarship. After my early mentors, particularly F. O. Matthiessen, Kenneth Murdock and Douglas
Bush, my long-range indebtedness is probably greatest
to the many students at the University of Connecticut
and Washington University (St. Louis) who taught as
well as listened for about fifteen years. More immediate
are my debts to the English Faculty of Oxford, and
particularly to Professors Norman Davis and Helen
Gardner and Miss Rachel Trickett, for the invitation to
lecture; to the officials in the United States and England
concerned with the Fulbright appointment; to Michigan
State University for a generous leave which made it
possible for me to accept the Fulbright, and for time
released from teaching duties that allowed me to finish the
manuscript; to the Warden and Fellows of All Souls for
hospitality in Oxford, and to members of the Depart-
ment of English at the University of California, Los
Angeles and the Librarians at the William Andrews
Clark Memorial Library, Los Angeles, for a fellowship
and a good summer's work.

Thanks are also due to the publishers for permission to

reprint some material. Chapter I has appeared in *The University of Toronto Quarterly*. The last pages of Chapter III have previously appeared as part of my Introduction to *The Selected Poetry of George Herbert* (New York and London: The New American Library and The New English Library, 1967); the discussion of Marvell's 'The Garden' in Chapter V appeared in *The Centennial Review*, Vol. XIII, No. 1 (Winter, 1969); and a few paragraphs in Chapter V and most of Chapter VI were included in an essay on Marvell published in the Stratford-upon-Avon Studies volume on *Metaphysical Poetry*, ed. Malcolm Bradbury and D. J. Palmer (London: Edward Arnold, 1970). I feel most personal debts to Miss Kathleen Lea, Mr Douglas Gray, and my wife as my faithful and most encouraging listeners at Oxford. The dedicatory pair must take a good deal of responsibility for initial influence and impetus, but none of course for the stupidities and mistakes.

December 4, 1968   EAST LANSING, MICHIGAN

THE HEIRS OF DONNE AND JONSON

CHAPTER I

The Heritage: Donne and Jonson

OVER fifteen years ago I wrote a long and intemperate footnote in which I objected to the use of the terms 'metaphysical poets' and 'metaphysical poetry':

The literary term 'metaphysical,' whether defined by 'spirit' or style, has lost whatever descriptive value it may once have possessed. Rarely used with much precision from Dryden on, it has in the last thirty years been loosely applied to various qualities and poems. Poets classified as 'metaphysical' have included Dante, Lucretius, Browning, and Wordsworth. Those essays and anthologies which have attempted to confine the term to a specific school in seventeenth-century England have rarely included identical figures as members of the 'school': Mark Van Doren used the adjective according to the statistical evidence of his bibliography when he remarked, 'By metaphysical poetry I mean the poetry of the seventeenth century.' The conception of the 'metaphysical conceit' offers small aid, since there is as little agreement in the definition of the noun as of the adjective: catachresis was used before Donne; the 'structural metaphor' has never been unknown to English poetry; and the degree of 'shock,' 'fantasticality,' or 'incongruity' in a metaphor can be measured only by a sense, possibly mistaken, of the poetic norm at any one period of time. Finally, thought and emotion are 'fused' to a greater or lesser degree in all good poetry. It would, therefore, seem in the interest of precise communication to avoid the word 'metaphysical' whenever possible. The following words, among others, convey most of the meanings intended by the term in the past: 'great,' 'passionate,' 'disillusioned,' 'sceptical,' 'intellectual,' 'rational,' 'philosophical,' 'theological,' 'sensual,' 'sensuous,' 'conversational,' 'anti-poetic,' and 'rough.'

Perhaps most useful, since it is so awkward it would not be abused, is 'Donne-like.'[1]

My vehemence derived from the fact that I was trying to understand the poetry of George Herbert and had found much of the then prevalent concern with the labeling and analysing of 'metaphysical' poets and poetry of limited helpfulness. I am not convinced that the adjective has generally been used with increased clarity or precision in the intervening years: the term has been extended to a large number of the continental poets of the sixteenth and seventeenth centuries; to Pope, Gray, Burns, Emerson, Thoreau, Whitman, Emily Dickinson, Hopkins, and Swinburne; to Goethe, Baudelaire, and Leopardi; and to practically every reputable twentieth-century poet, British or American—the difficulty today is to discover a poet who has *never* been called 'metaphysical.' Although Helen Gardner, in her fine anthology of 1957, *The Metaphysical Poets*, demonstrated that the term can still be used for intelligent and important literary discussion, I prefer to avoid it for a simple reason: I am interested in a number of seventeenth-century poets and I should like to understand more about their qualities and their range; the use of the term 'metaphysical,' however enlightened, almost inevitably results in an emphasis on the influence of Donne and one kind of poetry at the expense of other influences and kinds which I find of almost equal interest.

Critical and historical classifications are difficult anyway. We can hardly think at all without them, but unless we are very careful in our use of them, they may reduce our capacity for fresh experience. For my present purposes, the traditional categories suggested by Douglas Bush in his volume of the *Oxford History of English*

Literature, English Literature in the Earlier Seventeenth Century: 1600-1660,[2] may be most useful and least dangerous. Bush divided the poets of the period into what he called the 'successors' of Spenser, Donne, and Jonson, and he also noted that it was almost impossible to distinguish between the last two groups. Bush's word 'successors' may perhaps be just a bit overly-cautious in not implying quite enough. 'Followers,' with its suggestion of conscious discipleship, implies a good deal too much, as does 'school'—unless we can imagine a symposium with more than one teacher. After some hesitation, I have chosen 'heirs'—not with the implication that the later poets had any familial or natural rights or that either Donne or Jonson intended that they should inherit, but in simple recognition that they came to occupy a good deal of the literary estate of their two great predecessors. We are not, of course, usually much interested in literary heirs unless they are capable of developing their properties. And at the risk of destroying my metaphor, I think I should add that in the non-legal world of cloudy literary inheritances, it is not always profitable or possible to distinguish between appearance and reality.

The most important distinctions between the poetry of Donne and the poetry of Jonson approximate the differences which John Buxton has recently described between the kinds of poetry circulated in manuscripts among literary coteries in the 1590's and the kinds intended for publication:[3] poetry imitating private voices in contrast to poetry imitating public voices, poetry written by conscious amateurs in contrast to poetry written by professionals. Donne was the man who wrote, shortly after the publication of his 'Second Anniversary' in 1612, 'Of my Anniversaries, the fault that I acknowledge in my self, is to have descended to print any thing in verse, which though it have excuse even in our times, by men who professe, and practise much gravitie; yet I confesse I wonder how I declined to it, and do not pardon my self . . .'⁴; and Jonson was the man who shocked and amused his contemporaries by disclosing his literary seriousness and ambition when, four years after Donne's remark, he published some of his plays and poems as his *Works*.

From the major contrast implied, one can easily move to the popular contrast between 'colloquial' and 'formal' styles. But that formulation can be misleading. It may seem to postulate a single, completely unselfconscious, 'natural' (and therefore for some readers 'good') style, so close to an abstraction called 'reality' as to be its inevitable voice, and another, 'artful,' 'artificial,' 'rhetorical,' completely removed from any spoken language—and therefore 'bad.' I doubt that things have ever been that simple; at any rate, such a distinction is too crude for an age as rhetorically aware as the late sixteenth and early seventeenth centuries. It is possible to hold theoretically that 'real,' 'essential' man is man utterly alone, with no thought of others or of an audience, but it is hardly possible to talk sensibly about such a notion. Once we admit the use of language, that incorrigibly social medium, we are involved, willy-nilly, with matters of audiences, stances, purposes, and all the rest. *Every* use of language is more or less 'artful' or 'formal' as its user is more or less conscious of what he is doing and successful in doing it; and every use of language has also some relation (although sometimes a sadly remote one) to language as it has been either spoken or sung. 'Formal' and 'colloquial' alone strike me as too vague to be very useful: 'colloquial' for whom? what kind of speakers in what mood? speaking directly to whom? overheard by whom? for what purposes? And what kind of 'formality'? inviting what sorts of recognitions or participations from what readers or hearers? I do not mean to imply that these are easy questions or that I have the answers to them. (What *can* one determine about the 'audience' and 'purposes' of a persuasion to love, written both in a middle style and in the form of a strict Italian sonnet, addressed to a real lady but published by the poet?) But they are questions which we might keep in mind when we read Donne and Jonson and the rest. And it may be helpful also to question some of our perhaps unconscious assumptions about colloquialism and linguistic 'realism' in general. Is the heightened speech of a passionate persuasion to love more 'colloquial' than the fairly neutral conversation of old lovers—or of a husband and wife? Is speech addressed to one hearer necessarily more 'realistic' than speech addressed to several hearers? Is language expressing anger or impatience intrinsically more 'authentic' than meditative language—or even social chatter? Is harshness always more 'real' or even 'colloquial' than euphony?

In my following attempt to sketch briefly something of the heritage which Donne and Jonson left to their heirs, I shall treat Donne even more inadequately than Jonson, not because he is less important nor because I admire him less, but simply because he is generally better known and better read today. I can find no signs to indicate that Donne's achievement and influence are likely to be underrated. Despite some pious gestures and some good essays, I think most contemporary readers are likely to miss a good deal of Jonson's range and strength and art.

There are advantages in beginning with the epigrams and 'Paradoxes and Problems,' particularly since that seems to be about where Donne and Jonson began. Donne's few epigrams are off-hand squibs, most of them only two-lines long and many of them very funny; such as 'Antiquary':

> If in his study Hammon hath such care
> To'hang all old strange things, let his wife beware.

Or, 'A Selfe Accuser':

> Your mistress, that you follow whores, still taxeth you:
> 'Tis strange she should confess it, though'it be true.

In his recent edition, W. Milgate attributes to Donne 'Manliness':

> Thou call'st me effeminate, for I love women's joys;
> I call not thee manly, though thou follow boys.[5]

Jonson, by contrast, called his 'Epigrams' the 'ripest of my studies,' and published one-hundred-three; he included complimentary and elegiac as well as satiric epigrams and even expanded the term to include a scabrous mock-heroic of almost two-hundred lines, 'The Famous Voyage.' Jonson was usually serious about imitating (and attempting to surpass) Martial. In most of his epigrams he seems to have wanted a density, a deliberate and weighty judgement, a public and permanent status close to that of an actual inscription, even when they, too, contained only a single couplet:

> *To Alchemists*
> If all you boast of your great art be true;
> Sure, willing poverty lives most in you.   (No. VI)

More characteristic (and more impressive) are epigrams of eight or ten lines, such as 'On some-thing, that walks some-where':

> At court I met it, in clothes brave enough,
> To be a courtier; and looks grave enough,
> To seem a statesman: as I near it came,
> It made me a great face, I asked the name.
> 'A lord,' it cried, 'buried in flesh, and blood,
> And such from whom let no man hope least good,
> For I will do none: and as little ill,
> For I will dare none.' Good Lord, walk dead still.
>
> (No. XI)

What we are invited to admire here is less the cleverness of the observer than the justice and precision of his observation. The symmetries of the poem ('brave enough' and 'grave enough,' 'To be' and 'to seem,' 'good' and 'ill,' 'do' and 'dare'), carefully climaxed by the implied contrast between walking dead and being alive, help convince us that private judgement has, in fact, correctly observed public reality. Jonson often gains something of that effect, even in his most personal and moving epitaphs. He seems to have begun, if not as an aged eagle, at least with the tone of a sober and fully mature citizen. One could almost deduce his admiration for Francis Bacon and Selden.

The witty, mercurial, 'interesting' young man who speaks Donne's epigrams is, I think, more clearly defined in 'Paradoxes and Problems,' those prose juvenilia to which Donne devoted a good deal more care. He is, literally and quite intentionally, dazzling. He knows all the old arguments and can stand them on their heads. He is a master of wild analogy, semi-arcane lore, and false logic. He cannot only play the usual young man's game of hooting at generally accepted conventions and the gray-beards (by, for example, defending women's inconstancy or their duty to paint), but he can have even more sport in hoisting other such young men with their own petards: what fun to *defend* as paradoxes the notions that virginity is a virtue or that 'it is possible to find some virtue in some women'! And he is wonderfully inventive in thinking up multiple solutions for 'problems' such as 'Why Hath the Common Opinion Afforded Women Souls?' and 'Why doth the Pox so much Affect to Undermine the Nose?' The 'Paradoxes and Problems' are virtuoso performances. Our chief pleasure is in the agility of the intellectual footwork, the fertility of the invention, the gaiety of all that energy. The usual pose is scpetical, satirical, endlessly knowing; but if the young speaker has any settled or serious convictions it is all to his present purpose that they should not show. The last thing he wishes is to give a sense of mature, public, and permanent judgement. Donne's young speaker could not possibly be imagined as the author of any of Jonson's epigrams—only, perhaps, as the subject of one. Although both poets went on to different and more ambitious kinds of poetry, I think one can continue to catch glimpses in the poems of these early speakers' stances and assumptions and values.

The most substantial third of Jonson's epigrams are eulogistic. They evidence Jonson's conviction that part of the poet's duty was to provide the voice of fame for his worthy contemporaries (Jonson told Drummond that he meant to perfect 'an Epic Poem intitled Heroölogia,' a praise of the worthies of England) as well as his attempt to make eulogy more believable and more interesting than it often was. One way to praise a quality was to imitate or echo it. When Jonson addressed the usually mellifluous Francis Beaumont, for example, he used end-stopped couplets whose balanced construction conveys the compliment almost as clearly as does their meaning:

> How I do love thee Beaumont, and thy Muse,
>   That unto me dost such religion use!
> How I do fear my self, that am not worth
>   The least indulgent thought thy pen drops forth!
> At once thou mak'st me happy, and unmak'st:
>   And giving largely to me, more thou tak'st.
> What fate is mine, that so it self bereaves?
>   What art is thine, that so thy friend decieves?
> When even there, where most thou praisest me,
>   For writing better, I must envy thee.   (No. LV)

The three poems which concern Donne (largely as satirist and elegist) are very different. One addressed to Donne seems an allusion to, if not a parody of, Donne's 'masculine persuasive force,' with its reversed feet, harsh alliterations, arbitrary elisions, enjambment, and its blunt imperative:

> Who shall doubt, Donne, where I a poet be,
>   When I dare send my Epigrams to thee?
> That so alone canst judge, so'alone dost make:
>   And, in thy censures, evenly, dost take
> As free simplicity, to disavow,
>   As thou hast best authority, t'allow.
> Read all I send: and, if I find but one
>   Marked by thy hand, and with the better stone,
> My title's sealed. Those that for claps do write,
>   Let pui'nes, porters, players praise delight,
> And, till they burst, their backs, like asses load:
>   A man should seek great glory, and not broad.
>   (No. XCVI)

One does not have to believe that Jonson ever for a minute thought his title to poet depended on Donne's

opinion to recognize the seriousness of the poetic ambition which such epigrams imply. Jonson seems to have
believed that a poet should know and be able to imitate
the best contemporary poets and styles. Furthermore, as
the most thoroughgoing classicist England had yet produced, he believed that 'the true artificer' should be
mastercraftsman enough to provide a demonstration of
Milton's ideal of the well-educated man, by performing
'justly, skilfully, and magnanimously all the [*poetic*]
offices, both private and public, of peace and war.' For
Jonson such a demonstration included the composition of
the epigrams, the verse-letters, the odes, the songs, the
epithalamiums, the tragedies, the comedies, and those
masques which combined entertainment and compliment,
mythical fictions and social realities, as well as most of the
beautiful arts. It seems inevitable that Jonson should have
translated Horace's *Art of Poetry*. It is hard to imagine
Donne's doing so.

But however universal his theory, the most convinced
classicist must usually recognize some practical limitations
of temperament as well as of public and private circum-
stances. Donne's example underscores Jonson's limitations dramatically, since many of the things Donne did
best were things which Jonson attempted infrequently,
half-heartedly, or not at all: the satires, the personal or
dramatic love poems, and the divine poems.

It was surely public circumstance which prevented
Jonson, the poet who could hardly praise a man or a
house without giving a detailed account of the unattrac-
tive things it was not, who invented the antimasque, and
who spent some time in prison because passages in his
plays came too close to the powerful, from following
Donne's example in composing a book of *Satires*. It is

almost a shock to remember that the closest he came to
formal satire was in the verse letters, the epigrams, and
such trifles as 'A Satyrical Shrub' and 'A Little Shrub
Growing By' (*The Underwood*, XX and XXI). But the
satirical strain is rarely very far below the surface; its
usual tone varies from disdain and disgust to moral outrage. Jonson put his Juvenal on the stage in *Sejanus*.

Within his *Satires*, Donne gave the voice of his outrageous and witty young man a fully developed social and
dramatic context. And however much he suffers from the
fops and boors and fools on the street and at Court, his
descriptions of them are usually delightful. In *Satire*, I, the
speaker's description of his encounter with the 'fond-
ling motley humorist' is, in its movements, something
new:

> Now leaps he upright, jogs me,' and cries, 'Do'you see
> Yonder well favoured youth?' 'Which?' 'Oh, 'tis he
> That dances so divinely,' 'Oh,' said I,
> 'Stand still, must you dance here for company?'
> He droopt, we went, till one (which did excel
> Th' Indians, in drinking his tobacco well)
> Met us; they talked; I whispered, 'Let us go,
> 'T may be you smell him not, truly I do.'
> He hears not me, but, on the other side
> A many-coloured Peacock having spied,
> Leaves him and me; I for my lost sheep stay;
> He follows, overtakes, goes on the way,
> Saying, 'Him whom I last left, all repute
> For his device, in hansoming a suit,
> To judge of lace, pink, panes, print, cut, and plight,
> Of all the Court, to have the best conceit.'
> 'Our dull Comedians want him, let him go;
> But Oh, God strengthen thee, why stoop'st thou so?'
> 'Why? he hath travailed.' 'Long?' 'No, but to me'
> (Which understand none) 'he doth seem to be

Perfect French, and Italian.' I replied,
'So is the Pox.'   (ll. 83-104)

In the *Satires* Donne put narrative, dialogue, argument, and rapidly and erratically moving verses to the creation of an extraordinary sense of *this* moment, this scene, these odd people and their odder language. His central speaker is nearly always finely witty, but in his fearful alertness, the impatience of his responses, and the intemperance of his suffering, he often seems more of a participant than a judge of the satiric situation.

Absurdities of language, legal and religious jargon, courtier's or Coryat's crudities are of major concern in all of the *Satires* except *Satire* III, the best. That poem creates the speech of a man torn between tears and laughter, outraged by the usual confusion of mortal and immortal values and convinced of the necessity of seeking 'true religion'; and it ends with an attack on the wisdom, justice, and safety of anyone's mindlessly following an established religion, an attack which, I imagine, could hardly have been spoken with impunity before any monarch of the time. In that *Satire* Donne's young speaker becomes engaged with issues worthy of his deepest emotions, and both he and the verse are transformed. It seems quite proper that at the centre of the poem there should be an extended passage wittily describing wrong (and conventional) reasons for choosing a religion in terms of equally wrong reasons for choosing a wife or mistress, for the two subjects which touched Donne's imagination most intensely and provided the subjects for his best poems were sex and religion, the love of women and the love of God.

If Jonson held in theory that a poet should be able to

write exhaustively about almost everything, Donne came near to fulfilling such an ideal in practice on the one subject of the psychology of love. In his *Love Elegies* and *Songs and Sonnets*, the individual speaker sometimes loves all women and sometimes he curses or despairs of all or announces that he is through with love. Sometimes he says that he can love any woman, or any woman so long as she is true, or any woman so long as she is untrue. Sometimes he cares only for the woman's body and the physical act of love; on at least one occasion he claims to love only one woman's virtuous soul. In some of the best poems, he insists that love is properly fulfilled only when it embraces both body and soul. But before we conclude that these poems are direct reflections of one unusually varied sexual autobiography, we should notice that two of the poems are written in the voice of a woman, one of them arguing wittily for absolute female promiscuity ('Good is not good, unless / A thousand it possess').[6] In addition to their varied attitudes and speakers, the poems explore various forms of address (often, as Helen Gardner has suggested, owing something to Ovid, the classical epigrams, Petrarch, or the English drama): a lover advises other lovers on how best to begin an affair; he satirizes the foulness of another lover's mistress; he celebrates his new day of love as the beginning of a new life; he celebrates a full year of love; he imagines the future canonization of himself and his mistress as saints of a new religion of love; he laments the death of his loved one; he imagines his own burial; he makes his will. And he frequently explores the technically metaphysical (Neoplatonic or scholastic) subtleties concerning the nature and number of the new being which results from the perfect union of lovers. There are, however, some limitations. Helen Gardner has remarked that Donne 'never speaks in the tone of a man overwhelmed by what he feels to be wholly undeserved good fortune.'[7] I should think, too, that we value the note of simple tenderness in 'Sweetness love, I do not go' partly because it is so rare in Donne. And 'The Flea' is memorable, among other reasons, because it is one of the few occasions in which Donne used (and, I think, parodied) the traditional persuasion to love. It is almost as if Donne wished to explore all the possibilities of personal love poetry except the sort that had been most popular in the vernacular: the poem which declares initial passion or devotion and attempts to persuade the lady to respond. In nearly all of Donne's best love poems (and a number of them are surely among the best poems in the language), the speaker is either passionately engaged or outrageously witty and playful or both.

The contrast with Jonson is precise. Jonson began *The Forest* with 'Why I write not of Love':

> Some act of Love's bound to rehearse,
> I thought to bind him, in my verse:
> Which when he felt, 'Away' (quoth he)
> 'Can Poets hope to fetter me?
> It is enough, they once did get
> Mars, and my Mother, in their net:
> I wear not these my wings in vain.'
> With which he fled me: and again,
> Into my ri'mes could ne'er be got
> By any art. Then wonder not,
> That since, my numbers are so cold,
> When Love is fled, and I grow old.

The personal love poem, addressed by a recognizably individual speaker to a specific mistress (fictional or otherwise), is the realm of the amateur in more than etymology, and Jonson seems almost embarrassed by it. When he infrequently attempts such poems, he often presents himself as a ruefully comic figure. In 'My Picture Left in Scotland' (*The Underwood*, IX), for example, he attributes his failure in love to the notion that 'Love is rather deaf, than blind'; despite the excellence of his poems, he fears his mistress has seen

> My hundreds of gray hairs,
> Told seven and forty years,
> Read so much wast, as she cannot imbrace
> My mountain belly, and my rocky face,
> And all these through her eyes, have stopt her ears.

Even within his remarkable sequence 'A Celebration of Charis' Jonson presents himself as conscious that others see him as

> Cupid's Statue with a Beard,
> Or else one that played his Ape,
> In a Hercules-his shape.   (No. 3)

But a major Renaissance poet who could not write of love is almost inconceivable. The three Celia poems (*The Forest*, V, VI, IX) may economically suggest something of the way Jonson was able to write 'objective,' 'classical,' and also very English love poems. 'Drink to me, only, with thine eyes' may owe a great deal to Philostratus, but it is most remarkable in its successful anonymity. It is *the* English poem declaring a lover's secret pledge. As in many genuinely popular love poems, the speaker is characterized only by his emotion; any number of readers have been able to identify with him. The poem so completely expresses its situation that, as with the madrigals and lute songs and some popular modern songs, we feel little sense of impropriety of it is sung by a woman or by

27

more than one voice. 'Come my Celia, let us prove, /
While we may, the sports of love' is almost equally the
type of the cynical persuasion to love. The *carpe diem*
theme is even older than Catullus, but Jonson places and
criticizes the traditional arguments by the final lines:

> 'Tis no sin, love's fruit to steal,
> But the sweet theft to reveal:
> To be taken, to be seen,
> These have crimes accounted been.

Once the concepts of 'sin' and 'crimes' are openly
introduced into such a context, they cannot be easily dismissed. That Jonson hardly intended the poem to be
'persuasive' is suggested by its ironic context within
Volpone, where it first appeared: like Volpone's appeals to
erotic conspicuous consumption, the song is precisely
calculated to offend rather than to seduce a heavenly
Celia. 'Kiss me, sweet' is another matter still. Although
Catullus may again have furnished a point of departure,
the poem's request for a kiss expands to include a magnificent enumeration of local, natural, and English detail; and
when Jonson uses that sort of 'matter of England' in his
lyrics, we are usually invited not to judge but to rejoice:

> First give a hundred,
> Then a thousand, then another
> Hundred, then unto the other
> Add a thousand, and so more:
> Till you equal with the store,
> All the grass that Rumney yields,
> Or the sands in Chelsey fields,
> Or the drops in silver Thames,
> Or the stars, that guild his streams,
> In the silent summer-nights,
> When youths ply their stol'n delights.

The first stanza of 'Her Triumph,' that metrical *tour de force* from 'A Celebration of Charis' (*The Underwood*, II), suggests the other chief area of Jonson's success in love poetry: the masque, with all its visual, musical, and mythological resources:

> See the Chariot at hand here of Love
>> Wherein my Lady rideth!
> Each that draws, is a Swan or a Dove,
>> And well the Car Love guideth.
> As she goes, all hearts do duty
>> Unto her beauty;
> And enamour'd, do wish, so they might
>> But enjoy such a sight,
> That they still were to run by her side,
> Thorough Swords, thorough Seas, whither she would ride.

As some of their titles indicate (*Love Freed from Ignorance and Folly, Lovers made Men,* and *Love's Triumph through Callipolis,* for example), it is within the masques that Jonson used much of the traditional Renaissance lore concerning the 'philosophy of love.' It was Jonson who identified twelve types of depraved lovers and fifteen sorts of virtuous lovers (the latter number probably partly determined by the number of courtiers available for the occasion), and it was Jonson who anticipated both Milton and Dryden by occasionally writing of love in a new way:

> So love, emergent out of *Chaos,* brought
>> The world to light!
> And gently moving on the water, wrought
>> All form to sight![8]

No one would claim that Jonson's four 'devotional' poems are at all commensurate literarily with Donne's *Divine Poems.* To judge from his poetry, Jonson was not much concerned with theology, and he did not devote much of his life to religious meditation, There is nothing in Jonson to match the intensity of 'Batter my heart, three-personed God, 'the drama of 'At the round earth's imagined corners,' the imaginative intricacy of 'Good-friday, 1613. Riding Westward.' But although the best of Donne's *Divine Poems* are incomparable, their very qualities sometimes made for problems. [9] Sometimes, Donne had difficulty in constructing sestets which satisfactorily ful-filled the promise (or resolved the questions) of the usually brilliant octaves of his *Holy Sonnets*. And although it usually does not matter much if in reading a poem ad-dressed to a mistress a reader becomes much more interes-ted in the verbal play or a metaphor than in the subject or even in the speaker's attitude toward the subject, such distraction can sometimes be almost fatal to a poem addressed to God. In reading Donne's poems we are uncomfortably reminded at times of possible limits to the amount of individual, brilliant gymnastics which a benighted and repentant sinner can credibly display. Jonson's nearly 'anonymous' 'Hymn to God the Father' (*The Underwood*, I) manages the tone of humility more easily and convincingly than Donne usually does:

> Hear me, O God!
> A broken heart
> Is my best part:
> Use still thy rod,
> That I may prove
> Therein, thy Love.

And that single poem concludes with a sense of religious assurance which Donne hardly matched in his poetry except in his 'Hymn to God my God, in my sickness.'

But despite Jonson's differing sorts of successes, there can be little doubt of Donne's greater achievement as a love poet and as a sacred poet. It is within the public and semi-public poems, the verse letters (composed with varying degrees of formality, depending on the closeness of the friendships and the degrees of social distance), the 'epicides' and epithalamiums, the poems celebrating men or events, that Jonson's commitment to public voices and social judgements gives him a distinct advantage. In his verse letters (sometimes in the form of a sonnet) to close friends, Donne often exaggerated, with the greatest self-consciousness, his penchant for creating a harsh, idiosyncratic voice:

> I sing not, Siren-like, to tempt; for I
> Am harsh; . . . ('To Mr. S. B.: "O thou which to
> search out the secret parts" ')

> Now if this song be too'harsh for rime, yet as
> The Painter's bad god made a good devill,
> 'Twill be good prose, although the verse be evill,
> If thou forget the rime as thou dost pass.
> ('To Mr. T. W.: "All hail
> sweet Poet" ')

This can be good fun—although some readers have difficulty in remaining amused long enough to puzzle out the meter. (Jonson's remark that Donne deserved hanging for not keeping of accent was a precise one: Donne did usually 'keep' the proper number of syllables; but by a large amount of elision and the free substitution of feet, he sometimes reduced the expected iambic pattern of accents to an almost incredible fiction. Jonson's remark conveys a conscientious citizen's outrage that a rascal has successfully cheated without actually breaking the laws.) In those set pieces Jonson admired, 'The Storm' and 'The Calm,' Donne is masterly; his letter to Sir Henry

Goodyere is fine, and he is always near his best in the poems he addressed to Sir Henry Wotton. But in the letters to his Countesses (of Huntingdon, Bedford, and Salisbury), he is often at his worst. Those poems tend to overly-finespun ingenuities, slack quibblings, tedious lore. The limitless eulogy and the speaker's posture of rapt adoration are frequently distasteful. (If we feel this strongly, it may be because Donne's own better poems have taught us the ironic and self-limiting uses of such hyperbolic eulogy.) And, there are sometimes, too, grotesque lapses within Donne's more public attempts at eulogy or celebration. One is not at all surprised that Donne's 'Obsequies to the Lord Harrington' failed to please the Countess of Bedford, the dead man's sister. And it is difficult to imagine that the newlyweds of the 'Epithalamion Made at Lincoln's Inn' were any more pleased than the Countess when Death melodramatically entered the church during their wedding:

> Thy two-leaved gate's fair Temple unfold,
> And these two in thy sacred bosom hold,
>   Till, mystically joined, but one they be;
> Then may thy lean and hunger-starvèd womb
> Long time expect their bodies and their tomb,
>   Long after their own parents fatten thee.   (ll. 37-42)

Even stranger is that poem's climatic description of the bride's awaiting the bridegroom's approach, lying 'Like an appointed lamb, when tenderly / The priest comes on his knees t' embowel her.'

Just when one is about to conclude that Donne could not create and sustain a proper tone for a fully public poem, one remembers the Ecolgue and Epithalamion for the scandalous marriage of Robert Carr, Earl of Somerset, and Frances Howard, Countess of Essex, a long and ambitious poem which is consistently interesting and entertaining and which, so far as I can judge, contains not a single lapse, social or literary. Perhaps Donne carefully sought for and attained an adequate public tone because the political, social, and moral issues of that marriage were so delicate. (The poem may provide evidence in support of Donne's later remark, that in poetry 'I did best when I had least truth for my subjects.')[10] At any rate, Donne's poem surpasses, in both literary achievement and tact Jonson's verse-letter to Somerset upon the same occasion.[11]

Yet Donne's Eclogue and Epithalamion are not central to his work as most of Jonson's public poems are to his. It is within those poems that one can see, firmly related, Jonson's chief moral and poetic concerns. 'To Penshurst,' for example, like so many of Jonson's poems, is fundamentally a celebration of an ideal mean and measure—not merely an avoidance of extremes (whether of decoration or riches or emotion or individuality), but an orderly fulfilment of responsible actions within society, within the family, within the time of a human life. And the natural symbols for such a fulfilment come, of course, from the fruitful harvest of the elements and the year's cycle:

> The early cherry, with the later plum,
>> Fig, grape, and quince, each in his time doth come:
> The blushing apricot, and wooly peach
>> Hang on thy walls, that every child may reach.
> And though thy walls be of the country stone,
>> They're rear'd with no man's ruin, no man's groan,
> There's none, that dwell about them, wish them down;
>> But all come in, the farmer and the clown:
> And no one empty-handed, to salute
>> Thy lord, and lady, though they have no suit:

33

Some bring a capon, some a rural cake,
Some nuts, some apples; some that think they make
The better cheeses, bring 'hem; or else send
By their ripe daughters, whom they would commend
This way to husbands; and whose baskets bear
An emblem of themselves, in plum, or pear.

(The Forest, II, ll. 41-56)

'To Penshurst' creates, simultaneously, a moral ideal and an aesthetic which, relating value firmly to function rather than rarity or display, should have satisfied the theoreticians of the Bauhaus. The work of art is valued less for its memorial preservation of the past or its formal finish or completeness than for its continuing contribution to life:

Now, Penshurst, they that will proportion thee
With other edifices, when they see
Those proud, ambitious heaps, and nothing else,
May say, their lords have built, but thy lord dwells.

(ll. 99-102)

It is within such a context that we can best understand Jonson's remarks about language and style in *Timber*. 'Pure and neat Language I love, yet plain and customary.' '*Metaphors* farfet hinder to be understood, and affected, lose their grace.' 'The chief virtue of a style is perspicuity, and nothing so vicious in it, as to need an Interpreter.' 'That I call Custom of speech, which is the consent of the Learned; as Custom of life, which is the consent of the good.' Jonson attempted one of the most difficult things a poet can conceive in any age: to present an ideal of the mean, of rational control and fulfilled public function, so that it seizes the imagination of the reader and stirs his emotions. The clarity, the learning, and the labour were necessary for the successful communication of such an ideal; they also reflected it. Morevoer, some glimpses we

get of Jonson's temperament and actions (irascible, sometimes violent or drunken, dictatorial, professionally
jealous, occasionally crude in personal relations, satur-
nine, enjoying the exposure of the sordid) suggest that he
may have embraced both his ideal and the means to attain
it less because they were easily congenial than because
they were necessary for his survival. Jonson may have
been more temperamentally inclined to a despairing pessi-
mism than Donne. He seems to have found in his combination of a roughly neo-stoic ethic and a neo-classic
aesthetic a major sustaining force analogous to what Donne
discovered within the Church.

For a summary view of the differences involved in
Donne's and Jonson's approach to the public poem, one
might compare Donne's two *Anniversaries* on the death of
Elizabeth Drury with Jonson's 'To the Immortal
Memory, and Friendship of that Noble Pair, Sir Lucius
Cary, and Sir H. Morison' (*The Underwood*, LXX). I
think that the word 'marvellous' may be the correct one
for Donne's *Anniversaries*. Commissioned to honour the
memory of a young girl he had not known, Donne turned
her into a symbol of all the lost perfection of the world and
the poems into extraordinarily witty descants on two traditional themes: the anatomy of a corrupt world and the
progress of the souls of the blessed from this world to
the next. I differ from Professor Louis Martz in preferring
the *First Anniversary* to the *Second*.[12] I would agree that the
Second is more nearly unified and probably more serious
than the *First*, but I am not convinced that an anatomy
requires a high degree of unity nor that the quality of
religious meditation in the *Second* is greatly impressive.
And surely the *First Anniversary* is much the wittier of the
two. I find myself joining the responses of the man who

wrote the prefatory puffing poem for 'An Anatomy of the World' (probably Joseph Hall) both in his exclamation and in his formulation of the poem's fundamental paradox:

> Well died the World, that we might live to see
> This world of wit, in his Anatomy: . . .   (ll. 1-2)

> Yet how can I consent the world is dead
> While this Muse lives? which in his spirit's stead
> Seems to inform a World; and bids it be
> In spite of loss or frail mortality?   (ll. 7-10)

It would be difficult to discover elsewhere such spirited and inventive verse rushing so headlong to describe death, dissolution, and total decay:

> There is no health; Physicians say that we,
> At best, enjoy but a neutrality.
> And can there be worse sickness, than to know
> That we are never well, nor can be so?
> We are born ruinous: poor mothers cry,
> That children come not right nor orderly;
> Except they headlong come and fall upon
> An ominous precipitation.
> How witty's ruin: how importunate
> Upon mankind! it laboured to frustrate
> Even God's purpose; and made woman, sent
> For man's relief, cause of his languishment.
> They were to good ends, and they are so still,
> But accessory, and principal in ill;
> For that first marriage was our funeral:
> One woman at one blow, then killed us all,
> And singly, one by one, they kill us now.
> We doe delightfully our selves allow
> To that consumption; and profusely blind,
> We kill our selves to propagate our kind.   (ll. 91-110)

It is, I think, beside the point for us to spend much time wondering how suitable such a passage is for an elegy on a young girl or what the elder Drury's might have thought of it. And it is probably a mistake to object to the extravagance of the eulogy. Jonson thought that the poem was 'profane and full of Blasphemies' and told Donne 'if it had been written of the Virgin Mary if had been something,' but Donne answered that he did not describe a woman but the *Idea* of one. Granted that ideal perfection is what we have lost (always), we can rejoice in the wit and ingenuity with which the poem explores both the nature of perfection and the extremity of our own corruption.

> But she, in whom to such maturity
> Virtue was grown, past growth, that it must die;
> She, from whose influence all Impressions came,
> But, by Receivers' impotencies, lame,
> Who, though she could not transubstantiate
> All states to gold, yet guilded every state,
> So that some Princes have some temperance;
> Some Counsellers some purpose to advance
> The common profit; and some people have
> Some stay, no more than Kings should give, to crave;
> Some women have some taciturnity,
> Some nunneries some grains of chastity.
> She that did thus much, and much more could do,
> But that our age was Iron, and rustic too,
> She, she is dead; she's dead; when thou know'st this,
> Thou know'st how dry a cinder this world is.
> And learn'st thus much by our Anatomy,
> That 'tis in vain to dew, or mollify
> It with thy tears, or sweat, or blood: nothing
> Is worth our travail, grief, or perishing,
> But those rich joys, which did possess her heart,
> Of which she's now partaker, and a part.   (ll. 413-434)

Jonson's Pindaric ode on Cary and Morison is another matter. It seems to me one of the best and most 'serious' poems of the age. I would even defend its horrendous opening about the 'Infant of Saguntum' who, during the

37

siege of Hannibal, when half-born returned to his mother's womb to die. That bit of Senecan violence and even the fustian of 'Sword, fire, and famine, with fell fury met' both provide an analogy to Cary's and Jonson's and 'our' initial horror and near despair at the fact of the young Morison's death and help us to correct that response. For it is placed firmly with, 'could they but life's miseries fore-see, / No doubt all Infants would return like thee.' It *is* the proper response for infants; but the poem's primary concern is with an astonishing maturity which does not retreat from a world of violence and destruction and with a definition of life 'by the act' rather than 'the space' or simple duration. With the aid of negative examples (the old man who 'did no good' 'For three of his four-score' years, the one who makes his days seem years by repeating his fears and miseries, showing that he has 'been long, / Not lived') the poem leads us at last to rejoice in a vital triumph and fulfilment which time cannot touch. The central formuations of the moral measurement of life are presented triumphantly in terms which apply equally to the craftsman's successfully articulated poem:

> All Offices were done
> By him, so ample, full, and round,
> In weight, in measure, number, sound,
> As though his age imperfect might appear,
> His life was of Humanity the Sphere.   (ll. 48-52)

> . . . for life doth her great actions spell,
> By what was done and wrought
> In season, and so brought
> To light: her measures are, how well
> Each syllab'e answered, and was formed, how fair;
> These make the lines of life, and that's her ayre.
>
> (ll. 59-64)

In small proportions, we just beauties see:
And in short measures, life may perfect be. (ll. 73-74)

And such a force the faire example had,
As they that saw
The good, and durst not practise it, were glad
That such a Law
Was left yet to Man-kind;
Where they might read, and find
Friendship, in deed, was written, not in words:
And with the heart, not pen,
Of two so early men,
Whose lines her rolls were, and recórds.
Who e'er the first down bloomèd on the chin,
Had sowed these fruits, and got the harvest in.
(ll. 117-28)

At the centre of the formal celebration of this most neo-classic poem, Jonson was able to place himself, in person as well as name, almost playfully and more fully than he ever could have in a frankly confessional mode.

Considering these last poems and also some of Donne's finest *Songs and Sonnets* and *Divine Poems*, one is tempted to characterize the poetry of Donne and Jonson in terms of a whole series of seemingly opposed ideals and practices. Besides the private and the public, the amateur and the professional, the individual and the general, one thinks of extravagance and sobriety, excess and measure, spontaneity and deliberation, immediacy and distance, daring and propriety, roughness and elegance, tension and balance, agility and weight. And one can go on to expression and function, ecstasy and ethics, experience and thought, energy and order, the genius and the craftsman —ending with those inevitable seventeenth-century pairs, passion and reason, wit and judgement, nature and art.

39

But such a marshalling of abstractions can be misleading. So arranged, the members of those pairs may seem more fully antagonistic than they really are; and such an account obscures how much Donne and Jonson had in common. We should remember that three love elegies perhaps written by neither were attributed by contemporaries to both. A sentence from Douglas Bush suggests succinctly why such confusion was possible: 'Both poets rebelled, in their generally different ways, against pictorial fluidity, decorative rhetorical patterns, and half-medieval idealism, and both, by their individual and selective exploitation of established doctrines and practices, created new techniques, a new realism of style (or new rhetoric), sharp, condensed, and muscular, fitted for the intellectual and critical realism of their thought.'[13] Among a number of the things that Jonson said about Donne was the remark that he was 'the first poet in the world in some things'; and Donne addressed Jonson in a Latin poem as *Amicissimo et Meritissimo* and praised him as a unique kind of classicist, a follower of the ancients who dared to do new things. I think that each was correct in those judgements.

I shall frequently return to the poetry of Donne and Jonson as I discuss some of their heirs. There were, of course, valuable sorts of poetry for which neither Donne nor Jonson furnished adequate models, and the seventeenth-century poets were enormously fortunate to have Sidney, Spenser, and Shakespeare more or less readily at hand. Donne and Jonson's inheritance was less important as a fabulously rich collection of specific models than as a suggestion of the possibilities available for individual poets who were willing to explore varying, and even contrasting, speakers, modes, genres, and literary ideals.

CHAPTER II

Gentlemen of the Court and of Art:
Suckling, Herrick, and Carew

i

TO judge them by the standards of Sir Calidore or Sir Philip Sidney, neither Donne nor Jonson was quite a gentleman, in his poetry at least. In a number of his most successful poems, Donne consciously assumed the role of an upperclass anti-gentleman, seeing in traditional forms and ideals only barriers to individual desires and pleasures. Jonson's grandfather was a gentleman and his father a clergyman, but his stepfather was a bricklayer, and Jonson worked a while at that trade. Later, as a professional poet, he was beyond (I believe he thought above) the bounds of gentility. The aristocracy he was most concerned with was the aristocracy of the learned for the past two thousand years or so. He had friends among the gentlemen, he addressed them in epigrams and verse letters, and he gossiped about them; but his usual posture is that of a disinterested judge, able to give an expert opinion and concerned with maintaining proper standards. If anyone had dared to tell him that the language of his epistles or the speeches in his masques did not really very accurately represent the speech of contemporary English gentlemen, I think his response would have been close to that of Henry James in a similar encounter: 'So much the worse for them.'

Although it was largely from Donne's and Jonson's examples that a new ideal of proper gentlemanly literary expression was developed, the great exemplars did not really fulfil the new ideal either. Many of the ideas concerning love in Donne's *Songs and Sonnets* were thoroughly acceptable to the new gentlemen, but the speaker of them was usually too passionate as well as too learned—he cared too much. His open assertion of his ego dramatically asserted his needs, and beneath the surface of a number of Donne's poetic voices, a voice is crying, 'I want! I want!' The new ideal was usually that of a gentleman in moral as well as stylistic *déshabille*, but more nearly in control; he should be almost as superior to suffering as to any sexual attachments which restrained his freedom. The new gentleman (and perhaps one should really call him a Courtier, since he was often at Court) was beyond commitment and surprise and even ridicule, unless he gently and confidently directed the latter at himself. Jonson provided a model for much of the linguistic and metrical polish inevitably associated with such an ideal and for much else besides. But as a poet Jonson also cared too much and let his learning show. He was almost too elegant, often overly moral and serious, as well as laughably ambitious about being a poet.

I think we can best see the new ideal and its literary heritage in the poetry of Sir John Suckling—although the very clarity of both may distort, since hardly any other case is so obvious. Suckling helped establish the new tone, and he used it so well that even at the end of the century Congreve's Millamant could exclaim, 'Natural, easy Suckling.' She also exclaimed, 'filthy verses,' but she recognized that they were verses that told her a great deal about the ways of her world.

Suckling is conveniently informative about his ideals in 'A Sessions of the Poets.' The conscious doggerel of

that account of an imaginary contest for the laureate's
position is, I think, an initial suggestion of Suckling's
indebtedness to Jonson: it was Jonson who had, in his
plays and masques, explored the comic possibilities of
popular accentual rhythms and contemporary singing
commercials:

> A Sessions was held the other day,
> And *Apollo* himself was at it (they say),
> The Laurel that had been so long reserved
> Was now to be given to him best deserved.
>   And
> Therefore the wits of the Town came thither,
> 'Twas strange to see how they flocked together,
> Each strongly confidenct of his own way,
> Thought to gain the Laurel away that day.

A number of poets are present, but Jonson is the first to
speak:

> The first that broke silence was good old *Ben*,
> Prepared before with Canary wine,
> And he told them plainly he deserved the Bays,
> For his were called Works, where others' were but Plays.
>   And
> Bid them remember how he had purged the Stage
> Of errors, that had lasted many an Age;
> And he hopes they did not think the *Silent Woman*,
> The *Fox*, and the *Alchemist* outdone by no man.
>
> Apollo stopt him there, and bade him not go on,
> 'Twas merit, he said, and not presumption
> Must carry't, at which *Ben* turned about,
> And in great choler offered to go out:
>   But
> Those that were there thought it not fit
> To discontent so ancient a wit;
> And therefore *Apollo* called him back again,
> And made him mine host of his own new *Inn* (ll. 19-36)

43

Apollo's judgement was hardly consolatory for Ben; the signal public failure of *The New Inn* in 1629 was one of the sorest points in Jonson's career. The disorderly session ends with Apollo's crowning an alderman (on the good old grounds that if he is so rich he must be smart), but Suckling conveys the proper gentlemanly attitude towards the proceedings by describing his own response: he didn't attend:

> *Suckling* next was called, but did not appear,
> But straight one whispered *Apollo* i'th'ear,
> That of all men living he cared not for't;
> He loved not the Muses so well as his sport;
>
> And prized black eyes, or a lucky hit
> At bowls above all the Trophies of wit. . . .

'The Sessions' is amusing, and Suckling successfully sustains its tone of elaborate negligence. One of the most significant things about it is that Suckling mentions, in addition to himself and Jonson, twenty-two more-or-less gentlemanly poets who competed—omitting, incidentally, most of the poets with which I am here concerned. I do not mean to imply that Suckling only listed his cronies; the large group in attendance suggests rather an aspect of gentlemanly poetry in the early seventeenth century which we should not forget: that probably at no other time have so many Englishmen written at least one or two good poems.

Suckling also openly parodied Jonson. In 'A Celebration of Charis' (*The Under-Wood*, II), Jonson had ended his description of Love's Triumph with a stanza almost unsurpassed in its elegant sensuousness:

> Have you seen but a bright Lilly grow,
> Before rude hands have touched it?

> Ha' you marked but the fall o' the Snow
>   Before the soil hath smutched it?
> Ha' you felt the wool of Bever?
>   Or Swan's Down ever?
> Or have smelt o' the bed o'the Brier?
>   Or the Nard in the fire?
>   Or have tasted the bag of the Bee?
> O so white! O so soft! O so sweet is she!

Suckling turned that stanza on its head for a playful description of a very different kind of love:

> Hast thou seen the down i'th'air
>   When wanton blasts have tossed it,
> Or the ship on the sea
>   When ruder waves have crossed it?
> Hast thou marked the crocodile's weeping,
>   Or the fox's sleeping?
> Or hast viewed the peacock in his pride,
>   Or the dove by his bride
>   When he courts for his lechery?
> O, so fickle, O, so vain, O, so false, so false is she!

Suckling's uses of Donne are sometimes almost as obvious. He can frankly simplify the central idea of Donne's 'Love's Growth' for 'No, no, fair heretic, it needs must be,' or echo precisely the opening of 'Love's Deity.' Donne had begun,

> I long to talk with some old lover's ghost,
>   Who died before the god of Love was born:
> I cannot think that he, who then loved most,
>   Sunk so low, as to love one which did scorn.
> But since this god produced a destiny,
> And that vice-nature, custom, lets it be;
>   I must love her, that loves not me.

Suckling's 'Sonnet III' begins,

> Oh! for some honest Lovers ghost,
> Some kind unbodied post

45

Sent from the shades below.
I strangely long to know
Whether the nobler Chaplets wear,
Those that their mistress' scorn did bear,
Or those that were used kindly.

The way Suckling treats his model is fairly typical: Suckling's lines are shorter, his stanzas simpler in construction, his diction more ordinary. In the poem as a whole, Suckling substitutes for Donne's complex rhetoric and brilliant reversals, a casual expression of a single stance. After deploring Cupid's tyranny, Donne's speaker ends,

Rebel and Atheist too, why murmur I,
    As though I felt the worst that love could do?
Love might make me leave loving, or might try
    A deeper plague, to make her love me too,
Which, since she loves before, I'am loth to see;
Falsehood is worse than hate; and that must be,
    If she whom I love, should love me.

Suckling's speakers are rarely troubled by such logical and emotional shifts. *If* there is an Elysium for lovers, those who return each other's love must be together; so there can be no serious problem:

Some Bays (perchance) or Myrtle bough,
    For difference crowns the brow
    Of those kind souls that were
    The noble Martyrs here;
And if that be the only odds
(As who can tell?) ye kinder Gods,
    Give me the Woman here.

Occasionally Suckling's deliberate lowering of tension and temperament can paradoxically increase the sense of sexual brutality. In cold daylight, outside the context of the poems, the attitudes in Donne's poems are sometimes arrogant and callous; but they are so embedded in the brilliant rhetoric that they usually do not strike us as so: we are usually too much involved in the performance to take offence at the attitudes or manners or morals. In the *Songs and Sonnets* I think that only the final lines of 'Community' strike me as unpleasant in the Suckling fashion:

> Changed loves are but changed sorts of meat,
> And when he hath the kernel eat,
> Who doth not fling away the shell?

But if a poet who has rejected brilliant, learned, and 'engaged' effects writes poems asserting his indifference in matters of love, he is likely to shock us occasionally with brutality. Donne began 'The Indifferent' with an energetic and amusing stanza which includes its audience within its fiction:

> I can love both fair and brown,
> Her whom abundance melts, and her whom want betrays,
> Her who loves loneness best, and her who masks and plays,
> Her whom the country formed, and whom the town,
> Her who believes, and her who tries,
> Her who still weeps with spungy eyes,
> And her who is dry cork, and never cries;
> I can love her, and her, and you and you,
> I can love any, so she be not true.

The opening stanza of Suckling's adaptation ('Sonnet II') has its own genius:

> Of thee (kind boy) I ask no red and white,
> to make up my delight;
> no odd becoming graces,
> Black eyes, or little know-not-whats, in faces;

47

> Make me but mad enough, give me good store
> Of love for her I court:
> I ask no more,
> 'Tis love in love that makes the sport.

The stage shrug of that patronizing vocative to Cupid, 'kind boy,' seems to me very fine. (In its parody of elegant and bored sensuality, it reminds me of one of Hollywood's best moments, when Mae West turned to her maid with the remark, 'Mabel, peel me a grape.') But while Donne concludes 'The Indifferent' with an elaborate (and interesting) fiction, in which the first two stanzas are placed in the past tense (Venus has overheard the song, has conducted her own investigation of the claim that some women now want constancy in love, and proceeds to give her judgement in her own voice), Suckling's speaker merely repeats his indifference in an intentionally shocking manner:

> 'Tis not the meat, but 'tis the appetite
> makes eating a delight,
> and if I like one dish
> More than another, that a Pheasant is;
> What in our watches, that in us is found;
> So to the height and nick
> We up be wound,
> No matter by what hand or trick.

The ingenuity is not enough, I think, to redeem the ugliness.

The aesthetic problem (for the reader if not the poets) of how the new style gentleman could write of love without marring his effects with the sordid and brutal was to continue throughout the century. Lovelace, who is sometimes contrasted with Suckling to Suckling's disadvantage, did not find any real solution. When he was not striking noble and self-congratulatory poses in his few 'Cavalier' poems which have been so extraordinarily popular in the past hundred years or so (if they had not existed, the historical novelists would have had to invent them), Lovelace could be more shocking than Suckling, particularly when his elevated and low passages were crudely juxtaposed. Very few poets in the seventeenth century who wrote as much as Lovelace displayed such incompetence. One wonders sometimes whether he meant to say what he did, or even whether he always knew what he had said. According to all reports, he was extremely handsome and a great favourite with the ladies, and he wrote some brilliant phrases and lines ('Poor verdant fool! and now green ice!' of 'The Grasshopper,' 'Shake your head and scatter day' of 'To Amarantha,' or the opening of 'La Bella Bona Roba': 'I cannot tell who loves the skeleton / Of a poor marmoset, naught but bone, bone. / Give me a nakedness with her clothes on.') But he has little sense of structure and his syntax is sometimes shaky or hopelessly wrenched. He is also a small master of the mixed metaphor; 'To Lucasta. The Rose,' perhaps his outstanding achievement in that direction, seems clearly constructed with the expectation that if the images are pretty, the sense will take care of itself. And few poets in any age have attained the sheer mindlessness of a couplet from 'The Snail':

> Strict, and locked up, th' art hood all o'er,
> And ne'er eliminat'st thy door.

Edmund Waller (who has usually been underrated in our time) largely solved the literary problem of gentlemanly unpleasantness by heightening the formality of the voice of the speaker, placing him at some distance from his lady, and making him a master of euphony. But it was William Congreve who, in his prose comedies, at last placed the seventeenth-century amorous gentleman and his speech at the centre of complex and beautiful works of art. Congreve's achievement is a large subject; I wish only to remark in passing that whatever his hero's behaviour in the past, he is usually within the action of the play a gentleman who fully recognizes his irrational emotions and desires, and rationally sets out to satisfy them with urbane intelligence, nimbleness, imaginative sympathy, linguistic mastery—and the least possible pain to others.

Occasionally Suckling did not attempt a gentlemanly tone. His often-admired 'Ballad upon a Wedding' strikes me as an essay in an unfortunate genre: the consciously genteel imitation of quaint folksiness. Perhaps the poem might be considered a seventeenth-century manifestation of the *Oklahoma* syndrome—at any rate Suckling's arch countrymen speaking their stage Kentish are fairly precise equivalents to those cowboys and their Hollywood-Western lingo. When Suckling does make the voice of the new gentleman his own, as in 'Why so pale and wan, fond lover?' he is at his best. Another fine poem, however, suggests the way in which his very mastery helped to make his literary achievement seem less:

> Out upon it! I have loved
>   Three whole days together;
> And am like to love three more,
>   If it prove fair weather.
>
> Time shall moult away his wings,
>   Ere he shall discover
> In the whole wide world again
>   Such a constant Lover.

But the spite on't is, no praise
    Is due at all to me;
Love with me had made no stays,
    Had it any been but she.

Had it any been but she,
    And that very Face,
There had been at least ere this
    A dozen dozen in her place.

The easy tone and debonair exaggeration are just right: if gentlemanly colloquialism were the sole criterion for literary excellence, Suckling would be a major poet. But once learned, Suckling's tune could be easily reproduced; and there are hardly any limits to the literary possibilities of exaggerated inconstancy. Sir Tobie Matthews' answer to Suckling seems quite as good as the original:

Say, but did you love so long?
    In troth, I needs must blame you:
Passion did your Judgment wrong,
    Or want of Reason shame you.

Truth, Time's fair and witty Daughter,
    Shortly shall discover
Y' are a Subject fit for laughter,
    And more Fool than Lover.

But I grant you merit praise
    For your constant Folly;
Since you doted three whole days,
    Were you not melancholy?

She to whom you proved so true,
    And that very, very Face,
Puts each minute such as you
    A dozen dozen to disgrace.

ii

Robert Herrick seems to have wished very much to be a courtier.[1] He had some years in London when he knew some courtiers, he addressed a number of poems to royalty and the powerful (on one occasion getting a Duke's name wrong), he had some poems set to music by Henry Lawes and performed before the King at Whitehall, and he even accompanied Buckingham (as his chaplain) on the expedition to the Isle of Rhé. But that was about it. He had the disadvantage of not going up to Cambridge until the socially perhaps too-ripe age of twenty-two, he was ordained priest in 1623, and he spent most of his years (and his most productive as a poet) as vicar of a country parish in Devon. He constructed his own notions of proper speech largely on the elevated English model of Ben Jonson and on the poems of Anacreon, Catullus, Horace, Tibullus, Ovid, and Martial.[2] If one adds Seneca and the Bible, and, in English, Beaumont and Fletcher, Massinger, and that vast repository of curious lore, Robert Burton's *Anatomy of Melancholy*,[3] Herrick's most important literary inheritance is fairly fully suggested. Herrick is one of the few poets of the early seventeenth century who writes as though Donne had never written a poem—although he probably did know some of Donne's sermons.

The chief creative presence of Herrick's poetry is never for a moment in doubt: he is the most devoted (and the most single-minded) of the Sons of Ben, although he usually made use only of the epigrammatic and lyric part of the Jonsonian inheritance. He wrote four poems on Jonson's death: an elegiac epigram, an ode, a prayer, and

an epitaph. The opening couplet of the latter says it
simply enough:

> Here lies *Johnson* with the rest
> Of the Poets; but the Best.

His 'Prayer to Ben. Johnson' evidences both his mastery
of Jonson's lessons and a playfulness Jonson did not often
attempt:

> When I a Verse shall make,
> Know I have prayed thee,
> For old *Religion's* sake,
> Saint *Ben* to aid me.
>
> Make the way smooth for me,
> When I thy *Herrick*,
> Honouring thee, on my knee
> Offer my Lyric.
>
> Candles I'll give to thee,
> And a new Altar;
> And thou Saint *Ben*, shalt be
> Writ in my *Psalter*.

Jonson would not have invented that naïve voice which
both insists on the invocation of the saints of the old
religion and offers a bribe of a private canonization; but
he surely would have responded to the wit and delicacy of
'Honouring thee, on my knee / Offer my Lyrick.' We do
not have any very satisfactory way of talking about such
effects and, since critics and teachers have a way of preferring the things they can talk about best, they are often
underestimated. I think though, that such significant
movement is central to the art of poetry as Jonson and
Herrick understood it. To make that point, I have sometimes annoyed my students by suggesting that if they do

not recognize, for example, that in Jonson's song 'Queen and Huntress, chaste and fair' from *Cynthia's Revels* the line 'Goddess excellently bright' is a fine one, they might consider studying something besides English poetry.

In attempting to compare Jonson and Herrick, almost everyone eventually makes the comparison between the former bricklayer and the former goldsmith, the constructor of large social forms and the miniaturist or maker of filigree, the poet whom everyone called masculine and the one whom a number of readers have judged to possess a somewhat feminine sensibility. One can see the essential contrasts clearly enough in Herrick's adaptations of Jonson. For his masque *The Gypsies Metamorphosed* Jonson had written an impressive charm. (The 'firedrake' is the old fire dragon—probably either a meteor or a will-o'-the-wisp.)

> The faery beam upon you,
> The stars to glister on you,
>   A Moon of light
>   In the Noon of night,
> Till the firedrake hath o'ergone you.
>
> The wheel of *fortune* guide you,
> The Boy with the bow beside you
>   Run ay in the way
>   Till the bird of day
> And the luckier lot betide you.

I think the casualness of that reference to Cupid in 'The Boy with bow beside you,' like Milton's to the story of Proserpina in 'Which cost Ceres all that pain / To seek her through the world,' represents English neo-classicism at its best. Herrick's 'The Nightpiece, to Julia' expands his model to four stanzas; the way it transforms the

supernatural charm to a decorative invitation to a lady is
suggested by the first:

> Her Eyes the Glow-worm lend thee,
> The Shooting Stars attend thee;
> And the Elves also,
> Whose little eyes glow,
> Like the sparks of fire, befriend thee.

Herrick's transformation of the central motif of 'Still to
be neat,' a song from *Epicoene, or the Silent Woman*, is
more startling and more typical. Jonson had written an
elegant, courteous, and devastating masculine judgment
on feminine over-neatness. (As is usual in the seventeenth century, 'Still' means 'always.')

> Still to be neat, still to be drest,
> As you were going to a feast;
> Still to be powdered, still perfumed:
> Lady, it is to be presumed,
> Though art's hid causes are not found,
> All is not sweet, all is not sound.
>
> Give me a look, give me a face,
> That makes simplicity a grace;
> Robes loosely flowing, hair as free:
> Such sweet neglect more taketh me,
> Than all th' adulteries of art.
> They strike mine eyes, but not my heart.

Herrick's 'Delight in Disorder' describes not the process
of judgement on female dress and the attachments of the
heart, but an observer bewitched into wanton distraction
by disorderly (not to say messy) feminine attire:

> A sweet disorder in the dress
> Kindles in clothes a wantonness:
> A Lawn about the shoulders thrown
> Into a fine distraction:

An erring Lace, which here and there
Enthralls the Crimson Stomacher:
A Cuff neglectful, and thereby
Ribbands to flow confusedly:
A winning wave (deserving Note)
In the tempestuous petticoat:
A careless shoe-string, in whose tie
I see a wild civility:
Do more bewitch me, than when Art
Is too precise in every part.

I do not think it is possible to state categorically which is the better poem. Our individual preferences will depend on what we want most from poetry, perhaps on how long we have lived—and maybe even on the time of day. Jonson's is surely the more 'mature,' but I am by no means convinced that maturity is a universal desideratum for all poems and all occasions. Despite the explosion of Jonson's use of 'adulteries,' Herrick's poem is more rhetorically inventive, fanciful, and energetic. The attribution of the observer's emotional and imaginative responses to the personified details of the lady's costume may be a trick, but Herrick uses it beautifully and it enables him to place his speaker in a splendidly comic light. Both are fine poems.

However much he owes to Jonson, Herrick is more than an imitation or smaller Jonson. I make the point aggressively because it has been fashionable for some years to patronize or even denigrate Herrick's achievement. One can easily see what might support that fashion. Even at their best, the 2500 or so epigrams and lyrics of *Hesperides* and *Noble Numbers* are like bonbons in at least one respect: tasting too many at a sitting can result in severe discomfort. And even read in moderate numbers,

Herrick's poems often seem too facile, and some of them are silly as well as repetitious. Herrick is often afflicted with archness. To my taste, his vein of Oberon and the little people (which he may have got from Drayton) seems regrettable: the tiny details of the fairyfolk, like some of his pastoral details, can become embarrassingly self-conscious: I hardly see how any reader can keep from regretting what happens to the fruits from Jonson's *Penshurst*, for example, within Herrick's parody of Marlowe's 'Passionate Shepherd to His Love':

> In wicker-baskets Maids shall bring
> To thee, (my dearest Shepardling)
> The blushing Apple, bashful Pear,
> And shame-fac't Plum, (all simp'ring there).

(ll. 35-38)

His exercises in the grotesque can become uglier than I can enjoy, and I find most of his religious verse either dull or unconvincing. Although we have no right to judge the sincerity of Herrick's religious convictions, I think we can say that he was not able to communicate much sense of it within his poems. I find it hard to imagine a movement less appropriate to a sinner's fears than the one Herrick creates for 'To his angry God':

> Through all the night
> Thou dost me fright,
> And holds't mine eyes from sleeping;
> And day, by day,
> My cup can say,
> My wine is mixed with weeping.

But when we have granted all that, there are still so many fine poems left, some of them of a unique polish and perfection. 'The Farewell' and 'Welcome to Sack' are witty, neo-erotic mock-heroics—a difficult mode to bring off. A number of the epitaphs are beautiful, firm, and touching. 'The bad season makes the poet sad' is one of the few first-rate poems directly concerning the English civil war. 'To the virgins, to make much of time' is one of the best—and certainly the most popular—of English *carpe diem* poems. And even the self-consciously quaint is enjoyable when it is controlled and given point by the sort of playful technical masterly which Herrick shows, say, in his handling of the two-syllable lines and their rhymes in 'His grange, or private wealth':

Though Clock,
To tell how night draws hence, I've none,
A Cock,
I have, to sing how day draws on.
I have
A maid (my *Prew*) by good luck sent,
To save
That little, Fates me gave or lent.
A Hen
I keep, which creeking day by day,
Tells when
She goes her long white egg to lay.
A goose
I have, which, with a jealous ear,
Lets loose
Her tongue, to tell what danger's near.
A Lamb
I keep (tame) with my morsels fed,
Whose Dam
An Orphan left him (lately dead.)
A Cat
I keep, that plays about my House,
Grown fat,
With eating many a miching Mouse.

> To these
> A *Tracy* I do keep, whereby
> I please
> The more my rural privacy:
> Which are
> But toys, to give my heart some ease:
> Where care
> None is, slight things do lightly please.

Herrick tends to be at his best when he is celebrating festivals, English or Latin or natural (Jonson may have suggested the direction; 'Ceremonies for Christmas' and 'Ceremonies for Candlemas Eve' are examples), and when he is writing of evanescence. The word 'superficial' may be justly applied to much of Herrick's poetry, but it is one of Herrick's strengths rather than weaknesses that this is so.[4] Herrick is continually concerned both with the surfaces of natural and human beauty and with the linguistic surfaces of his poems. And he is concerned often in a special way with the intricacies of appearances, the subtleties of surfaces and what they suggest: lawn, silk, crystal, cream, water, skin as they partially or momentarily reveal a lady's body, a lily, strawberries, pebbles, blood, and bone. A man who so loves the surface beauties of this world almost inevitably comes to feel the poignant brevity of such beauty and of this life. That is the subject of 'To daffodils,' one of Herrick's loveliest poems:

> Faire Daffodils, we weep to see
> You haste away so soon:
> As yet the early-rising Sun
> Has not attain'd his Noon.
> Stay, stay,
> Until the hasting day
> Has run

But to the Even-song;
And, having prayed together, we
Will go with you along.

We have short time to stay, as you,
We have as short a Spring;
As quick a growth to meet Decay,
As you, or any thing.
We die,
As your hours do, and dry
Away,
Like to the Summer's rain;
Or as the pearls of Morning's dew
Ne'er to be found again.

The poet who celebrates such beauty and states his acceptance of its evanescence is also, of course, attempting to stay, or to defeat, or to redeem the work of time.

Herrick's masterpiece, 'Corinna's going a Maying,' one of the two richest English embodiments of the classical *carpe diem* (the other is Marvell's 'To his Coy Mistress') shows all of his best themes and strains— often juxtaposed:[5] the goddess Aurora and an English 'sweet-Slug-a-bed,' 'Dew-bespangling Herb and Tree' and 'Fresh-quilted colours.' All religions sanctify this English fetching in of May and love: Apollo is present; 'Each Flower has wept, and bowed toward the East'; 'all the Birds' have said English Mattens and 'sung their thankful Hymns'; a 'thousand Virgins' are in attendance; 'Devotion gives each House a Bough, / or Branch,' and 'Each porch, each door' becomes 'An ark, a Tabernacle,' a booth both Hebrew and Roman constructed of English whitethorn; and the Priest is ready for the betrothal cere- monies. The conventional restrictive religious attitudes are reversed or subordinated to this central bidding to the rites of spring: "'tis sin, / Nay, profanation to keep in'; 'Wash, dress, be brief in praying: / Few Beads are best, when once we go a Maying'; 'And sin no more, as we have done, by staying; / But my *Corinna*, come, let's go a Maying.' And everything blooms or buds or becomes green: 'the Blooming Morn,' 'Rise; and put on your Foliage, and be seen / To come forth, like the Spring-time, fresh and green; And sweet as *Flora*'; each street becomes 'a Park / Made green, and trimmed with trees'; 'There's not a budding Boy, or Girl, this day, / But is got up, and gone to bring in May.' Nature and man are for a moment one. And, after all those imperatives ('Get up, get up for shame,' 'Get up,' 'Rise,' and the continually repeated 'Come') the final stanza firmly places time's inevitable prospect on this imperative to life and love:

> Come, let us go, while we are in our prime;
> And take the harmless folly of the time.
>> We shall grow old apace, and die
>> Before we know our liberty.
>> Our life is short; and our days run
>> As fast away as does the Sun:
> And as a vapour, or a drop of rain
> Once lost, can ne'er be found again:
>> So when or you or I are made
>> A fable, song, or fleeting shade;
>> All love, all liking, all delight
>> Lies drowned with us in endless night.
> Then while time serves, and we are but decaying;
> Come, my *Corinna*, come, let's go a Maying.

Herrick's best poems show what a Jonsonian concern with 'how well / Each syllab'e answered and was formed how fair' could mean for a relatively isolated poet enamoured with dreams of Rome and Merry England.

Their speech (of the epigrams and verse-letters and odes as well as the lyrics) is closer to the careful measure and euphony of song than to any spoken language of either passionate individuals or debonair courtiers. But Herrick's art, like Watteau's, is no less valuable because its usual world is remote, idealized, and fragile.

iii

With Thomas Carew we are back at the Court.[6] A brilliant and dissolute young man of good family, Carew acted as secretary to ambassadors in Italy and France, was later favourite of both King Charles and Queen Henrietta, and was given minor positions at Court in 1630. He died of syphilis in 1640 at the age of 45, virtually disowned by his parents, refused the sacrament and absolution by his friend John Hales, who had granted both on an earlier occasion when Carew thought he was dying. Such a brief account may cast too deep and idiosyncratic a shadow on the earlier gaiety. Suckling died even younger, supposedly a suicide at the age of thirty-three in 1642, but his early gaiety retains its own reality. (It is remarkable, however, how many of the group once known as the 'Cavalier Poets' either died before Charles raised his standard or took no active part in the Civil War.) In the earlier and happier days Suckling criticized his older friend for being too serious, too imaginative, and for working harder than was proper for a courtly poet. In 'A Sessions of the poets,' Suckling wrote,

> *Tom Carew* was next, but he had a fault
> That would not well stand with a Laureate;
> His Muse was hard bound, and th' issue of's brain
> Was seldom brought forth but with trouble and pain.

62

And
> All that were present there did agree,
> A Laureate Muse should be easy and free. . . .

In 'Upon My Lady Carlisle's Walking in Hampton Court Garden,' Suckling constructed a dialogue between himself and Carew. It begins with Tom:

> Didst thou not find the place inspired
> And flowers, as if they had desired
> No other sun, start from their beds,
> And for a sight steal out their heads?
> Heard'st thou not music when she talked?
> And didst not find that, as she walked
> She threw rare perfumes all about,
> Such as bean-blossoms newly out,
> Or chafèd spices give?—

And Suckling answers,

> I must confess those perfumes, Tom,
> I did not smell; nor found that from
> Her passing by aught sprung up new:
> The flowers had all their birth from you;
> For I passed o'er the self-same walk,
> And did not find one single stalk
> Of any thing that was to bring
> This unknown after-after-spring.

Tom.
> Dull and insensible, couldst see
> A thing so near a deity
> Move up and down, and feel no change?

And Suckling answers with a comic reduction:

> None and so great were alike strange.
> I had my thoughts, but not your way;
> All are not born, sir, to the bay. . . .

Suckling's affable criticism may indicate exactly why Carew seems today one of the most interesting of seventeenth-century poets. He *did* care about poetry; he was imaginative as well as witty; and he worked at it. He was also a most conscious heir of both Donne and Jonson :[7] he wrote one of the best critical evaluations of Donne (one of the best literary criticisms in English verse of anybody) and a reproof to Jonson which is so completely Jonsonian in its precision, measure, 'justice,' and values that it must have made Jonson wince.

In 'An Elegy upon the death of the Dean of Pauls, Dr John Donne,' Carew showed an ability to imitate the literary and poetic qualities he praised which makes Jonson's epigram to Donne seem slight. Early in the poem Carew devoted a remarkable passage to the power and method of Donne's sermons, in support of the notion that Donne had dispensed 'Through all our language, both the words and sense':

> The Pulpit may her plain,
> And sober Christian precepts still retain,
> Doctrines it may, and wholesome Uses frame,
> Grave Homilies, and Lectures, But the flame
> Of thy brave Soul, (that shot such heat and light,
> As burnt our earth, and made our darkness bright,
> Committted holy Rapes upon our Will,
> Did through he eye the melting heart distill;
> And the deep knowledge of dark truths so teach,
> As sense might judge, what phansie could not reach;)
> Must be desired for ever.   (ll. 11-21)

But most of the poem is reserved for the Donne which meant most to Carew, Donne the revolutionary innovator in secular poetry:

> The Muses' garden with Pedantic weeds
> O'rspred, was purged by thee; The lazy seeds
> Of servile imitation thrown away;
> And fresh invention planted. Thou didst pay
> The debts of our penurious bankrupt age;

Licentious thefts, that make poetic rage
A Mimic fury, when our souls must be
Possest, or with Anacreon's Extasy,
Or Pindar's, not their own; The subtle cheat
Of sly Exchanges, and the juggling feat
Of two-edged words, or whatsoever wrong
By ours was done the Greek, or Latin tongue,
Thou hast redeemed, and opened us a Mine
Of rich and pregnant phansie, drawn a line
Of masculine expression, which had good
Old Orpheus seen, Or all the ancient Brood
Our superstitious fools admire, and hold
Their lead more precious, than thy burnished gold,
Thou hadst been their Exchequer, and no more
They each in other's dust, had raked for Ore.
Thou shalt yield no precedence, but of time,
And the blind fate of language, whose tuned chime
More charms the outward sense; Yet thou may'st claim
From so great disadvantage greater fame,
Since to the awe of thy imperious wit
Our stubborn language bends, made only fit
With her tough-thick-ribbed hoops to gird about
Thy Giant phansie, which had proved too stout
For their soft melting Phrases.   (ll. 25-53)

One hopes not to sound too much like Polonius if one
remarks that this is good. Those marvellously energetic
run-over couplets, the quick and imaginative changes of
both rhythms and images, the imitation of rough and
masterful masculinity are evidence of Donne's still-living
poetic genius. (As with Donne's *First Anniversary*, the
very brilliance of the poem makes paradoxical its central
thesis that the glory has all departed.) But with all the
detailed knowledge, appreciation, and imitation of Donne
which the elegy shows, Carew is by no means here a
simple disciple. He laments that Donne's 'strict laws will

be / Too hard for Libertines in Poetry,' who will recall 'the goodly exiled train / Of gods and goddesses, which in thy just reign / Was banished nobler Poems,' but as one reads the poem one begins to wonder whether it is 'goodly exiled' or 'goodly train.' At any rate, Carew generally seemed to have little desire to banish them, and they are present: Donne's 'Promethean breath' kindled the fire of the 'Delphic choir' and there are the 'Muses' garden' and 'good / Old Orpheus.' The poem becomes a most classical 'crowne of Bays' to be burnt on Donne's 'funeral pile,' and it concludes with an epitaph to be 'incised' on the tomb whose form, at least, Jonson should have admired:

> *Here lies a King, that ruled as he thought fit*
> *The universal Monarchy of wit;*
> *Here lie two Flamens, and both those, the best,*
> *Apollo's first, at last, the true God's Priest.*

Carew's verse-letter to Jonson is subtitled, 'Upon occasion of his Ode of defiance annext to his Play of the new Inn.' When Jonson published the play in 1631, he included after the title the following: 'A Comedy. As it was never acted, but most negligently played, by some, the King's Servants. And more squeamishly beheld, and censured by others, the King's Subjects. 1629. Now, at last, set at liberty to the Readers, his Majesty's Servants, and Subjects, to be judged. 1631. By the Author, B. Jonson.' And at the end he printed a sixty-line poem with the note, 'The just indignation the Author took at the vulgar censure of his Play, by some malicious spectators, began this following Ode to himself.' It is the one beginning, 'Come leave the loathed Stage / And the more loathsome Age,' and it is not a very elevating performance: the public swine prefer husks and scraps ('a mouldy Tale, / Like Pericles' or 'Broome's sweepings'):

> 'Twere simple fury, still thy self to waste
> On such as have no taste.   (ll. 13-14)

It is always a bit embarrassing when one hears disappointed playwrights crying that a failure is all the fault of the actors, the critics, and the tasteless public; it is doubly so when the playwright is Jonson. Carew begins:

> 'Tis true (deare *Ben*): thy just chastizing hand
> Hath fixt upon the sotted Age a brand
> To their swol'n pride, and empty scribbling due,
> It can nor judge, nor write, and yet 'tis true
> Thy comic Muse from the exalted line
> Toucht by thy *Alchemist*, doth since decline
> From that her zenith, and foretells a red
> And blushing evening, when she goes to bed,
> Yet such, as shall out-shine the glimmering light
> With which all stars shall gild the following night.
> Nor think it much (since all thy Eaglets may
> Endure the sunny trial) if we say
> This hath the stronger wing, or that doth shine
> Trickt up in fairer plumes, since all are thine;
> Who hath his flock of cackling Geese compared
> With thy tuned choir of Swans?

The plays *do* differ in characteristics as well as quality:

> Though one hand form them, and though one brain strike
> Souls into all, they are not all alike.
> Why should the follies then of this dull age
> Draw from thy pen such an immodest rage
> As seems to blast thy (else immortal) Bays,
> When thine own tongue proclaims thy itch of praise?
> Such thirst will argue drouth. No, let be hurled
> Upon thy works, by the detracting world.
> What malice can suggest; let the rout say,
> The running sands, that (ere thou make a play)

Count the slow minutes, might a *Goodwin* frame
To swallow when th'hast done thy ship-wrackt name.
Let them the dear expence of oil upbraid
Suckt by thy watchful Lamp, that hath betrayed
To theft the blood of martyred Authors, spilt
Into thy ink, whilst thou growest pale with guilt.
Repine not at the Tapers' thrifty waste,
That sleeks thy terser poems, nor is haste
Praise, but excuse; and if thou overcome
A knotty writer, bring the booty home;
Nor think it theft, if the rich spoils so torn
From conquered Authors, be as Trophies worn

(ll. 21-42)

Jonson should stick to his principles, moral and literary: his independence, his painstaking craftsmanship, his study and appropriation of the best authors (midnight oil makes for sleek poems; minor poets borrow, while major ones steal). And Jonson should confidently trust the judgement of time; only he himself could injure his reputation —and he may have done so by descending to quarrel with his manifest inferiors:

The wiser world doth greater Thee confess
Then all men else, than Thy self only less.

The praise is so exact and so extreme that one might almost take the criticisms, like Cordelia's, as the checking of dangerous folly which love requires, were it not also so public—and without the excuse of dramatic necessity.

Carew's demonstrated knowledge and mastery of both Donne's and Jonson's poetry surpasses, I think, that of any other poet up to 1640. And Carew often surpasses Donne in the evocation of sensuous and sensual (rather than dramatic) immediacy. Donne's 'Ecstasy' is a remarkably intellectual performance, and his 'To his

Mistress Going to Bed' and 'Love's Progress' are more
notable for their wit and rhetorical playfulness ('Oh my
America, my new found land!') than for either sensuous
beauty or suggestiveness. It was in just those latter
qualities that Carew seemed determined to surpass the
Roman and Italian amorists—with no sacrifice of the wit
—when he wrote 'The Rapture,' his best-known poem
in his own time. And Carew sometimes surpasses Jonson
in courtly elegance and decorative compliment. How
much he owes those achievements to his own temperament and how much to French and Italian poetry (particularly to Marino, a number of whose poems Carew
translated and whom he may have known in Paris) is
impossible to determine. One can, however, see not only
his mastery of some effects of Donne and Jonson but also
his departures from their practice almost everywhere in
the lyrics:

> Now that the winter's gone, the earth hast lost
> Her snow-white robes, and now no more the frost
> Candies the grass, or casts an icy cream
> Upon the silver lake or crystal stream.
>
> ('The Spring')

> Mark how the bashful morn, in vain
> Courts the amorous Marigold
> With sighing blasts and weeping rain;
> Yet she refuses to unfold.
> But when the Planet of the day
> Approacheth with his powerful ray,
> Then she spreads, then she receives
> His warmer beams into her virgin leaves.
>
> ('Boldness in Love')

> I'll make your eyes like morning suns appear,
>   As mild, and fair;

69

> Your brow, as crystal smooth, and clear,
> And your dishevelled hair
> Shall flow like a calm region of the air.
> ('To a Lady that desired I would love her,' ll. 26-30)

> Give me a storm; if it be love,
> Like *Danäe* in that golden shower,
> I swim in pleasure. . . .'
> ('Mediocrity in love rejected')

Occasionally Carew's wit and ingenious compliment strike the modern reader as both excessive and offensive. It is hard to believe that his elegy on Maria Wentworth could have satisfied anyone's notions of decorum. It begins,

> And here the precious dust is laid;
> Whose purely-tempered Clay was made
> So fine, that it the guest betrayed.
>
> Else the soul grew so fast within,
> It broke the outward shell of sin,
> And so was hatched a Cherubin.

And it goes on, after an enumeration of the young girl's virtues, to

> So though a Virgin, yet a Bride
> To every Grace, she justified
> A chaste polygamy and died.

It may be a salutory check to our confident knowingness to be reminded that the girl's parents were evidently so pleased that they had the first eighteen lines (including those quoted) engraved on her tomb.

But twentieth-century and seventeenth-century taste are likely to agree about the masterly (and laboriously achieved) union of beauty, polish, and intellectual wit in Carew's most popular song:

> Ask me no more where *Jove* bestows,
> When *June* is past, the fading rose:
> For in your beauties' orient deep,
> These flowers as in their causes, sleep.

And I think most modern tastes would approve also of 'To my friend G. N., from Wrest,' a poem which, with 'To Saxham,' represents Carew's contribution to the group of English country-house poems deriving from Jonson's 'To Penshurst.' Carew praises Wrest Park, the Bedfordshire manor house of the De Greys, Earls of Kent, not as the fruitful emblem of the measured and responsible aristocratic life, but as the substantial fulfilment of the sensuous pleasures for which (according to the poem) all the myths are only remote and barren symbols:

> *Amalthea's* Horn
> Of plenty is not in effigy worn
> Without the gate, but she within the door
> Empties her free and unexhausted store.
> Nor, crowned with wheaten wreaths, doth *Ceres* stand
> In stone, with a crook'd sickle in her hand:
> Nor, on a marble tun, his face besmeared
> With grapes, is curled unscissored *Bacchus* reared.
> We offer not in Emblems to the eyes,
> But to the taste, those useful Deities.
> We press the juicy God, and quaff his blood,
> And grind the Yellow Goddess into food.
> (ll. 57-68)

The mundane fishes, swan, waterman, and boat in the double-moat at Wrest are envied by their analagous constellations in the heavens,

> which wish to slake
> Their star-burnt-limbs, in our refreshing lake,
> But they stick fast nailed to the barren Sphere,
> Whilst our encrease in fertile waters here

71

Disport, and wander freely where they please
Within the circuit of our narrow seas.   (ll. 83-88)

'To G. N., from Wrest' was probably Carew's last poem. It is useless to spend much time regretting that a minor poet never quite became a major one. ('It might have been' are very probably the silliest rather than the saddest words in literary criticism and history.) Besides, not many English poets wrote as many fine poems as Carew did. Still, some of those poems promise so much, Carew's technical equipment is so brilliant and so varied, that I can hardly resist such thoughts when I read Carew. T. S. Eliot once remarked that a poet's technical equipment should be 'like a well-oiled fire engine,' kept in first-class condition, ready for immediate use when the call to the fire came.[9] It seems that for Carew the call never came—or, perhaps, that the fires were fairly small.

I suppose that a major fire is simply a cause or occasion which demands all a poet's abilities and, for a moment at least, requires total imaginative commitment. For Herrick's finest moment it was merely a fresh vision of the old *seize the day*. With Carew one wishes, most naïvely, to join the cry from *Paradise Lost*, 'O for that warning voice!', when one hears him consider the possibility of a heroic subject or major commitment and refuse it. When Aurelian Townshend wrote an 'Elegiacal Letter' to Carew asking him to compose a poem on the death in late 1632 of Gustavus Adolphus, King of Sweden, Carew refused, less because the subject was unsuited to his 'Lyric feet' than because it was unsuited to the age in England. Germans may worry about political and military matters,

But let us that in myrtle bowers sit
Under secure shades, use the benefit

72

> Of peace and plenty, which the blessèd hand
> Of our good King gives this obdurate land,
> Let us of Revels sing. . . .   (ll. 45-49)

And the poem ends with,

> But these are subjects proper to our clime.
> Tourneys, Masques, Theaters, better become
> Our *Halcyon* days; what though the German Drum
> Bellow for freedom and revenge, the noise
> Concerns not us, nor should divert our joys;
> Nor ought the thunder of their carabins
> Drown the sweet Aires of our tuned violins;
> Believe me friend, if their prevailing powers
> Gain them a calm security like ours,
> They'll hang their arms up on the olive bough,
> And dance, and revel then, as we do now.
>   (ll. 94-104)

One does not have to remember that England was to be torn apart by civil war within ten years to recognize that such a smugly insular assumption of prosperity and an eternal party, like dancing on a volcano, was a defiance of the gods and fate which would have given pause to most Greeks and Romans. And in his skilful praise of George Sandys' translation of the Psalms, Carew proposed an elaborate intellectual 'What if?' about the possibilities of the conversion of himself and his muse from the love of women to the love of God:

> Perhaps my restless soul, tired with pursuit
> Of mortal beauty, seeking without fruit
> Contentment there, which hath not, when enjoyed,
> Quencht all her thirst, nor satisfied, though cloyed;
> Weary of her vain search below, Above
> In the first Fair may find th' immortall Love.
> Prompted by thy example then, no more
> In moulds of clay will I my God adore;

73

But tear those Idols from my heart, and write
What his blest Sp'rit, not fond Love shall indite. . . .

(ll. 23-32)

The poem does not state the refusal, but its language clearly implies the unreality of the proposal:

Then, I no more shall court the verdant Bay,
But the dry leaveless Trunk on *Golgotha*;
And rather strive to gain from thence one thorn,
Than all the flourishing wreaths by Laureats worn.

(ll. 33-36)

There is surely little danger that anyone will become a religious poet who conceives of the decision only as the choice between a 'dry leaveless Trunk' and greenness.

The grandest public occasion to demand Carew's talents was answered by his masque, *Coelum Britannicum*,[10] designed and produced by Inigo Jones and presented before the King at Whitehall on Shrove Tuesday, 1634. Sir Henry Herbert, George Herbert's younger brother, Master of the Revels since 1623, called it 'the noblest masque of my time to this day, the best poetry, best scenes, and the best habits,' and the Queen remarked (in French) that she had never seen such fine costumes. Based on a philosophic dialogue, *Spaccio de la Bestia Trionfante*, which Giordano Bruno had dedicated to Sidney, the masque is brilliant, witty, outrageous, and suggests the end of an age. Where, after all, could the complimentary court masque go after it had described and shown, with the aid of *eight* antimasques and a scurorilus prose Momus, Jupiter's decision to clean out the old, scandalous constellations from the heavens; Mercury's exposure of the claims of Riches, Poverty, Fortune, and Pleasure to replace them; and the British Genius's provision of new constellations in the figures of Charles I's

74

courtiers? (The production of *Comus* the following Michaelmas suggested a transformed genre and a new society.) The passage in Carew's masque which I find most impressive and most touching (and which Carew did not get from Bruno) is Mercury's neo-Spenserian rejection of Hedone, or Pleasure, after her claims of sovereignty ('Beyond me nothing is, I am the goal, / The journey's end, to which the sweating world, / And wearied Nature travels') and her masque of the five senses. It suggests, I think, that Carew, like some later poets, had come to know by experience that a simple sensuous hedonism may be one of the most painful of all creeds, particularly for a man past thirty-five, but that it was about all he had:

> Bewitching Syren, guilded rottenness,
> Thou hast with cinning artifice displayed
> Th' enameled outside, and the honied verge
> Of the fair cup, where deadly poison lurks.
> Within, a thousand sorrows dance the round;
> And like a shell, Pain circles thee without,
> Grief is the shadow waiting on thy steps,
> Which, as thy joys 'gin tow'rds their West decline,
> Doth to a Giant's spreading form extend
> Thy dwarfish stature. Thou thy self art Pain,
> Greedy, intense Desire, and the keen edge
> Of thy fierce appetite, oft strangles thee,
> And cuts thy slender thread; but still the terror
> And apprehension of thy hasty end,
> Mingles with gall thy most refinèd sweets;
> Yet thy *Circean* charms tranform the world.
>
> (ll. 809-824)

CHAPTER III

Gentlemen at Home and at Church:
Henry King and George Herbert

HERRICK, Carew, George Herbert, and Henry
King were the four most distinguished poets born
in the early 1590's. Unlike the others, King never
seems to have desired a career at Court.[1] Born into a
family with a strong clerical tradition, he was early destined to a career in the church; but although he became
one of the chaplains in ordinary to the King, he never
seems to have aspired to the power and influence which
his father, the bishop who ordained his old friend John
Donne, obtained in the see of London. Henry King lived
most of the time in London (with a minor office at St.
Paul's and the Archdeaconry of Rochester) until well past
the age of forty-five, when he was made Dean of Rochester.
In 1641, he was elected Bishop of Chichester, supposedly
as a sop to the anti-Laudian faction; his consecration came
early in 1642, the day after the Bishops were deprived of
the vote in the House of Lords, and within less than a year
of the Act for the abolition of the episcopacy. King was
restored to his hardly-ever-enjoyed bishopric in 1660, but
by that time he was sixty-eight, and he had long ceased
writing poetry. He died in 1669. I believe that King's
unusual youthful ambition and his clerical ambience
partly account for some of the individual qualities of his
poetry.

With King, as with all the other poets, I am chiefly
concerned with the individual qualities: what he made of
what he received. But this may be a good place to be

reminded that the things the seventeenth-century poets shared were not matters simply of *literary* tradition or influence—or, perhaps, that the literary was inextricably involved with a social world which was smaller and more intimate than anything that we are likely to know. It sometimes seems that in the England of the time, there was more cause for explanation if two poets did not know each other than if they did. London, the great metropolis, contained, according to Douglas Bush's estimates, 'somewhat less than 250,000 people in 1600 and somewhat more than 400,000 in 1660.'[2] With the continuing power and influence of a few families and institutions, the literary world seemed relatively smaller still. If, for example, you take the 'Sidney connexion' and, say, Donne's and Jonson's Countess of Bedford, Lucy Russell, you really can say that they were friends to, relations of, or patrons to most of the significant writers of the late sixteenth and early seventeenth centuries. Margaret Crum has remarked, in her excellent edition of King's *Poems*, on the large number of poets who attended Westminster School, including (in order of their dates of birth) William Alabaster, Ben Jonson, Richard Corbet, Giles Fletcher the Younger, Henry King, George Herbert, William Strode, Thomas Randolph, William Cartwright, Abraham Cowley, and John Dryden. Miss Crum suggests that such an astonishing list may have something to do with the fact that boys in the top forms at Westminster 'were sometimes set to turn "Latin and Greek verse into English verse".'[3] One also remembers Jonson's expression of indebtedness to Camden—and for more than his practice of writing his first drafts in prose. When one considers too how many of the Westminster poets-to-be went on to Trinity College, Cambridge (Alabaster, Fletcher,

77

Herbert, Randolph, Cowley, and Dryden) and that they were joined there by Sir John Suckling (who Aubrey said had also been at Westminster) and by Andrew Marvell, it seems possible that the practice of poetry may have been somewhat contagious, that the more distinguished practitioners one knew well or recognized as colleagues or family connections, the more likely one would try one's hand seriously at the craft.

King's life supports that notion. While he was still a child he came to know Donne, and they became friends despite the twenty years' difference in their ages. If any poet deserved to be called the heir of Donne it was King, for Donne left him his notes and intended him as the literary executor for the works he wished to be published, the sermons.[4] There is odd evidence, too, that King was considered an heir of Jonson: left-over sheets of his poems were reissued in 1700 as *Ben Jonson's Poems, Elegies, Paradoxes and Sonnets*. Although we are accustomed to the desperate expedients publishers sometimes take to move a slow seller, it does seem strange that this publisher expected his buyers to believe that Jonson had written an elaborate funeral elegy for himself. King showed his allegiance and his loyalty in an elegy for Donne as well as one for Jonson. He joined Carew in praising George Sandys' *A Paraphrase upon the Divine Poems*; unlike Carew, however, he did not at all think the age too happy to attempt an elegy for Gustavus Adolphus, and in some lines of his he even touched successfully the heroic strain.

These are among the large number of King's poems, mostly elegiac, in celebration of public occasions. It seems the fashion to dismiss them, but I must confess to affection for a number of them. They are usually slow, often repetitious, and sometimes dull; but they are also usually

78

sensible, adequate to their occasions, and they sometimes possess fine passages. I have to admit, however, that if these were all, we should probably be no more interested in King than in a dozen other poets of the time. King's elegy on Donne ends with a splendid couplet in illustration of the thesis that only Donne was worthy or able to praise Donne properly:

> So jewellers no art, or metal trust
> To form the diamond, but the diamond's dust.

But up until that point, King's poem, unlike Carew's on the same occasion, never really places in doubt its central argument that the startling glory of the language has departed.

King tried a number of forms besides the public elegies, congratulations, and celebrations. The opening lines of 'A Letter' seem almost to parody the blunt epistolary persona which Jonson sometimes assumed:

> I ne'er was drest in forms; nor can I bend
> My pen to flatter any, nor commend,
> Unless desert or honour do present
> Unto my verse a worthy argument.

He wrote some epigrams, two paradoxes, and some 'sonnets'—usually brief stanzaic poems (none of fourteen lines) such as 'The Vow-Breaker' or 'The Double Rock' more or less in the manner of Donne, and others which are nearer to the Jonsonian lyric: 'Tell me no more how fair she is' is one of the most graceful poems of the age. And he also tranlated the Psalms for singing to the old tunes. But almost any reader is struck less by the variety of forms and modes within the body of King's verse than by the general prevalence of the valedictory subject and tone, whether mortuary or amatory. Perhaps even more noteworthy is the fact (or at least I believe it to be a fact) that in most of the best poems and even passages the voices and audiences are distinctive: either the poet seems to speak in his own domestic voice as if to members of his immediate family or he disappears as an individual within the intentionally 'anonymous' or collective voice of reasonable or just or contemplative men.

Douglas Bush has estimated that two-fifths of King's poems are of the obituary variety.[5] The fact that for about forty-five years, from the death of Prince Henry in 1612 to that of Lady Katherine Cholmondeley, Countess of Leinster, in 1657, he marked a number of his public and private losses with elegies accounts for a large number of them. But that custom does not explain why in a congratulatory poem on the birth of Prince Charles in 1630 he should choose to emphasize the birth of an heir as a reminder of the parents' mortality:

> in age or fate, each following birth
> Doth set the parent so much nearer Earth:
> And by this grammar, we our heirs may call
> The smiling Preface to our Funeral.   (ll. 23-26)

Nor does it account for poems on such general subjects as 'An Essay on Death and Prison,' 'An Elegy Occasioned by Sickness,' 'My Mid-Night Meditation,' or 'The Dirge.' There are also a whole group of poems on the sad farewells of lovers: 'The Surrender,' 'I prithee turn that face away,' 'The Farewell,' 'The Retreat,' 'The Forlorn Hope,' and 'The Change.' Two poems, 'The Departure' and 'An Acknowledgment,' each over fifty lines in length, concern the farewells and separation of friends. Most strange of all are two valedictories either for or to what seem to be totally imaginary persons and situations: a paternal elegy 'On two Children dying of one Disease, and buried in one Grave' and 'The Legacy,' in which the poet anticipates his leavetaking from a younger, second wife. (Although this poem, along with the attribution to Henry King of some poems written by his brother John, has caused scholars to invent a second wife for the occasion, Miss Crum's investigations seem to establish that she never existed.[6]) After reading these, one feels it was inevitable that King should have written an epitaph on Niobe.

Although most of the poems which King addressed, in his own person, to the commendation or memory of public figures seem among his least interesting, when he wrote in anger and political partisanship—and necessarily more or less anonymously—he could extend his elegiac strain to include forceful and impressive satire. Both the poem on the death of Essex and the elegy on the deaths of Sir Charles Lucas and Sir George Lisle (executed on Fairfax's order after the siege of Colchester) are among the most impressive poems to come out of the Civil War. It is not merely a matter of emotional commitment or personal involvement. No one can doubt the sincerity of 'A Deepe Groan, fetched at the Funeral of that incomparable and Glorious Monarch, Charles the First, King of Great Britain, France, &c. On whose Sacred Person was acted that execrable, horrid, & prodigious Murther, by a traitorous Crew and bloody Combination at Westminster, January the 30, 1649,' which seems King's immediate response to the death of Charles and was published in two editions and reprinted in 1649. But although King tries to write it as if he is reflecting 'our' collective response, he is unable to control his personal horror. The poem is extravagant, shrill, and occasionally almost incoherent; the overwhelming sincerity of the poet's immediate emotion may have actually proved a handicap to the later reader's attempts to imagine or share that emotion But a number of years later, from a fuller perspective on his own responses partly provided by his judgements on later political developments, King wrote a long, remarkably impressive 'Elegy upon the most Incomparable King Charles the First' in which the horror and the fierceness are under effective control. A passage addressed to the Parliamentarians may represent King's 'anonymous' satire at its finest:

> Yet have You kept your word against Your will,
> Your King is Great indeed and Glorious still,
> And You have made Him so. We must impute
> That Lustre which His Sufferings contribute
> To your preposterous Wisdoms, who have done
> All your good Deeds by Contradiction:
> For as to work His Peace you raised this Strife,
> And often Shot at Him to Save his Life;
> As you took from Him to Encrease His wealth,
> And kept Him Pris'ner to secure His Health;
> So in revenge of your dissembled Spite,
> In this last Wrong you did Him greatest Right,
> And (cross to all You meant) by Plucking down
> Lifted Him up to His Eternal Crown.   (ll. 463-76)

King's devastating catalogue of the old slogans indicates that unspeak was invented long before *1984*. In those lines, King has already abandoned Donne's notions of satire for the sort of clarity, balance, and ironic point which were to characterize the satire of a new age.

King's usual elegiac tone is quite different. Ordinarily he hardly raises his voice in his calm and sometimes witty expressions of resignation. He is, as one couplet expresses it, 'Content . . . to Lament,'[7] whether particular individals or imaginary loves or the condition of man. And anyone who thinks that such a stance (never an enormously popular one) is always inadequate for good poetry should consider what King's skill in metaphor, rhythmic control, and rhetorical variations made of the popular *Sic Vita* theme. The model for a number of English variations seems to have been a 12-line poem, probably written either by Simon Wastell or Francis Quarles, which in its mechanical construction and rhythm suggests remarkably few poetic possibilities:

> Like as the damask rose you see;
> Or like the blossom on the tree;
> Or like the Sun; or like the shade;
> Or like the gourd which Jonas had;
> Even such is man, whose thread is spun.
> Drawn out, and cut, and so is done.
>> The rose withers; the blossom blasteth;
>> The flower fades; the morning hasteth;
>> The sun sets; the shadow flies;
>> The gourd consumes; and man he dies.[8]

That poem can serve as a useful reminder of the sort of artless, semi-popular verse that was produced in abundance during the period. King transformed it into a beautiful and moving work of art:

> Like to the falling of a star;
> Or as the flights of eagles are;
> Or like the fresh Spring's gaudy hue;
> Or silver drops of morning dew;
> Or like a wind that chafes the flood;
> Or bubble which on water stood;
> Even such is Man, whose borrowed light
> Is straight called in, and paid to night.
>> The wind blows out, the bubble dies;
>> The Spring, entombed in Autumn lies;
>> The dew dries up: The star is shot:
>> The flight is past: and Man forgot.

But it is in the poem which everybody knows, 'An Exequy to his Matchless never to be Forgotten Friend,' written on the occasion of his wife's death in 1624, that King achieved the triumph both of his elegiac strain and his intimate or domestic style. 'Intimate' and 'domestic' do not imply for King disorder or unrestrained emotion or, even, lack of formality or wit. A seventeenth-century man might argue that it is exactly in the home and in familial relations that control, wit, and a degree of formality are most useful and even necessary for the proper expression of our consideration for those we love. The fact that King addressed his 'Exequy' directly to his dead wife did not at all imply that he forgot what he had learned at Westminster and Christ Church and in the pulpit concerning rhetorical method. He constructed a most elaborate and artful schema for the poem: an opening address to the body ('thou Shrine of my Dead Saint') requesting that the poem ('this Complaint') may be accepted 'Instead of dirges' or 'sweet flowers to crown thy Hearse'; a long meditation addressed to her ('Dear Loss!' 'Loved Clay!') in a conversational tone concerning his grief, his loss, and his inability to view her again until the Judgement; an ironic address to Earth, threatened as a rival who temporarily possesses his love by means of a legally limited lease; an extraordinary couplet addressed to the gravediggers, as if the time of the poem and the time of the procession and burial were actually one ('So close the ground, and 'bout her shade / Black curtains draw, My Bride is lay'd'); and the final address to 'my Love,' the 'last Good-night,' which both assures her that he is already on his way to join her and asks her pardon for his willingness to live. Within that artificial scheme, the language and the couplets are witty, playful, and even when most moving almost as natural as breathing. I can think of no earlier lines of Renaissance poetry which capture this sort of domestic tone so poignantly unless they are Desdemona's to Emilia in Act IV, Scene iii of *Othello*, that most domestic of Shakespeare's tragedies. The last lines suggest the ease, the wit, the tenderness, and the magic. Their mock-pompous reproof to the subordinate for not observing 'just precedence' is very close to Montague's reproof to Romeo: 'O thou untaught! What manners is in this, / To press before thy father to a grave?'

> 'Tis true; with shame and grief I yield
> Thou, like the van, first took'st the field,
> And gotten hast the victory
> In thus advanturing to die
> Before me; whose more years might crave
> A just precedence in the grave.
> But hark! My pulse, like a soft drum
> Beats my approach, tells thee I come;
> And, slow howe'er my marches be,
> I shall at last sit down by thee.
>   The thought of this bids me go on,
> And wait my dissolution
> With hope and comfort. Dear! (forgive
> The crime) I am content to live
> Divided, with but half a heart,
> Till we shall meet and never part.   (ll. 105-20)

I cannot leave King without citing one other poem. Not at all an elegy (although it shows King's elegiac hallmark: the recurrent placing of the major cadence after the third, fourth, or fifth syllable rather than at the end of the line), it seems to me another triumph of the domestic tone and the middle muse. The title is fully explanatory: 'To my Sister Anne King who chid me in verse for being angry':

Deare Nan! I would not have thy counsel lost,
Though I last night had twice so much been crosst:
Well is a passion to the market brought,
When such a treasure of advice is bought
With so much dross. And could'st thou me assure
Each vice of mine should meet with such a cure,
I would sin oft, and on my guilty brow
Weare ev'ry imperfection that I owe,
Open and visible. I should not hide
But bring my faults abroad, to hear thee chide
In such a note, and with a quill so sage
It passion tunes, and calms a tempest's rage.
   Well I am charmed; and promise to redress
What, without shrift, my follies do confess
Against my self. Wherefore let me entreat
When I fly out in that distempered heat
Which frets me into fasts, thou wilt reprove
That froward spleen in poetry and love.
So though I loose my reason in such fits,
Thou'lt rhime me back again into my wits.

It may have been that a combination of his own temperament and his life away from even much thought of the
Court transformed Henry King's poetic heritage. At any
rate, I think his most remarkably individual achievement,
evident also in a number of his shorter poems, was the
creation of a verse and tone proper, not for public uses
or gentlemanly coteries or for either high drama or self-
assertion or display, but for the most inimate personal and
familial uses.

   Unlike Henry King, his classmate at Westminster, for
quite some time George Herbert hoped to attain a position
of importance at Court.[9] When Reader in Rhetoric at

Cambridge he expounded on the speeches of King James as models of oratory far surpassing those of the ancients. Later, when he was Latin Orator, there was a time, according to Walton, that he 'enjoyed his gentile humor for clothes, and Court-like company, and seldom look'd towards *Cambridge*, unless the King were there, but then he never failed.'[10] Only when he was thirty-three did he signal the end of that hope by taking deacon's orders; and he was not ordained priest until he was thirty-seven, less than three years before his death.

Both Herbert's mother and his older brother, Edward, Lord Herbert of Cherbury, were close friends of Donne's. Donne addressed poems to Magdalene Herbert and preached her funeral sermon, and both Donne and Jonson exchanged complimentary verses with Edward Herbert (although Jonson maliciously reported that Donne told him he had written his 'Epitaph on Prince Henry' 'to match Sir Edward Herbert in obscureness'). As Latin Orator George Herbert devoted a number of elaborately ornamental poems in Latin or Greek to the praise of individuals: King James, Bishop Andrewes, Prince Henry, Prince Charles, Queen Anne, a number to Bacon, a slim volume to commemorate his mother's death, and a Latin epigram responding to one of Donne's, to which he seems to have appended two brief epigrams on Donne's death.[11] It is remarkable, then, that his English poems should differ so entirely: aside from translations of the Latin epigrams to and on Donne and a couple of doubtful epitaphs, none of his surviving English poems mentions a single other living human being. In them, too, there is astonishingly little trace of the English poetry that Herbert read: a few obvious uses of Sidney, some arguable phrases and metaphors and one unquestioned line from Donne, what seems to be a use of Southwell, and a parody of a poem by his distant cousin, William Herbert, third Earl of Pembroke. I think also that Herbert's poem 'Discipline' suggests an indebtedness to Jonson's 'A Hymn to God the Father' in style as well as tone and subject, but it would be difficult to prove. Such meticulous care to avoid human eulogy and the verse-letter as well as the easier and more obvious sorts of literary imitation are evidence of Herbert's deliberate decision to address his best English poetry, sometimes indirectly but usually directly, to an unusual rhetorical audience: God. Like King, Herbert turned away from the usual audiences of classicists, wits, and gentlemen, but his achievement was both more striking and more important. *The Temple* is the best and wittiest collection of religious lyrics in English; and its impact on mid-seventeenth-century Englishmen, Laudians and Puritans, royalists and parliamentarians, readers and poets alike, was large. Helen Gardner has suggested that it was the first volume of lyrics in English for which each poem was carefully provided a significant title by its author.[12] In the use of titles as in other ways one can see *The Temple*'s influence on the volumes that followed. The rash of volumes containing only serious devotional poems (instead of mixing the secular and the sacred in the earlier fashion) seems to derive as specifically from the stimulus of the publication of *The Temple* in 1633 as the rash of sonnet sequences in the 1590's derived from *Astrophil and Stella*.

Herbert divided *The Temple* into three sections, 'The Church-porch,' 'The Church' (the main body of over one-hundred-sixty shorter poems), and 'The Church Militant,' a long and rather strange 'prophetic' poem about the westward movement of both the Church and Sin until the

Day of Judgement. It is the poems within the central
section, 'The Church,' which are the great ones; but,
although it discourages most modern readers, I think
Herbert knew what he was doing when he prefaced them
by a 462-line didactic poem. For if his young contemporaries, like, say, the Thomas Carew who had accompanied
Edward Herbert to Paris in 1619 as one of the gentlemen
attendants on the new ambassador, or even George
Herbert's younger brother, the Sir Henry who later
admired Carew's masque so extravagantly, were to read
and to respond to Herbert's devotional poems in the way
he wished, they would need a good deal of preparation,
literary as well as religious, for the experience. In 'The
Church-porch,' Herbert put the traditional, classical (and
Jonsonian) mixture of pleasure and profit to the uses of
Christian didactic verse.

In the first stanza Herbert makes unmistakable the
audience he has in mind for the poem:

> Thou, whose sweet youth and early hopes enhance
> Thy rate and price, and mark thee for a treasure;
> Hearken unto a Verser, who may chance
> Rhyme thee to good, and make a bait of pleasure.
> A verse may find him, who a sermon flies,
> And turn delight into a sacrifice.

He conceives of a reader (significantly addressed in the
singular rather than the plural) who is a worldy young
man of the contemporary ruling class. He assumes his
intelligence, his pleasure in verse and wit, and his more-
or-less-enlightened self-interest. He also assumes that the
reader would wish neither to offend others nor to mar his
own chances for worldly advancement. (Well along in the
poem, the speaker remarks, 'Who say, I care not, those I
give for lost; / And to instruct them, will not quit the

cost.' They would, at any rate, be unavailable to prudential argument.) The young gentleman is assumed to know the conventional Christianity of his time and to appreciate common-sense arguments, but not at all to be consumed by the love of God.

Herbert organized his seventy-seven stanzas largely by skilful use of traditional methods. The stanza which immediately follows the introductory address begins with 'Beware of lust,' not, I think, because lechery is the chief or even the most common sin nor because it is Herbert's personal obsession, but because Herbert wishes to begin with the least important of the Deadly Sins, lechery and gluttony, the sins of the flesh, and will proceed through the sins more directly affecting society, sloth, and avarice, to finally, the greatest spiritual sins of anger, envy, and pride. The traditional ordering is so embellished that few readers seem to have noticed its existence. Between the stanzas concerning drunkenness and those about sloth, for example, there are five on the misuses of language—boasting about sins 'in wine or wantonness,' swearing, and lying. They make the transition from fleshy to social vanity clear, remind us of Christ's admonition that it is 'that which cometh out of the mouth' which 'defileth a man,' (Matthew xv, 11) and also include two of the Ten Commandments. Moreover, the stanzas concerning sloth expand to include the cause of English sloth (improper education), and the proper building of character. These lead into stanzas on self-discipline and the establishment of rules and habits—a natural transition, again, to the dangers of avarice and then to the proper management of money. The warnings against anger and envy are buried within a large section on conversation, laughter, and wit. Herbert is anything but hobbled by the traditional. He emphasizes the virtues opposing the Deadly Sins, and the Aristotelian as well as the traditional Christian virtues. The two groups of stanzas just before the brief conclusion concern the giving of alms and public worship, those manifestations of the love of our neighbours and the love of God. At the end of the poem, the 'sweet youth' has been brought to church.

Along the way he has been consistently engaged and often entertained. One of the chief pleasures available to such poetry derives simply from the recognition of memorable formulations of traditional wisdom:

> Gold thou mayst safely touch; but if it stick
> Unto thy hands, it woundeth to the quick.
>
> (ll. 167-68)

> None is so wasteful as the scraping dame.
> She loseth three for one: her soul, rest, fame.
>
> (ll. 173-74)

> Man is God's image; but a poor man is
> Christ's stamp to boot: both images regard.
>
> (ll. 379-80)

We are reminded of Herbert's large collection of 'outlandish' or foreign proverbs. With proverbial wisdom safely on the side of virtuous behaviour, the obvious corollary which Herbert underlined was the stupidity of evil:

> Drink not the third glass, which thou canst not tame,
> When once it is within thee; but before
> Mayst rule it, as thou list; and pour the shame,
> Which it would pour on thee, upon the floor.
> It is most just to throw that on the ground,
> Which would throw me there, if I keep the round.
>
> (ll. 25-30)

91

Surely one should practice a little self-interest? Herbert's impatience with the gentry's sloth occasioned a fine apostrophe, a passage which Aldous Huxley considered both accurate and prophetic concerning the gentry's 'bleats':[13]

> O England! full of sin, but most of sloth;
> Spit out thy phlegm, and fill thy breast with glory:
> Thy Gentry bleats, as if thy native cloth
> Transfused a sheepishness into thy story:
>   Not that they all are so; but that the most
>   Are gone to grass, and in the pasture lost.
>
> This loss springs chiefly from our education.
> Some till their ground, but let weeds choke their son:
> Some mark a partridge, never their child's fashion:
> Some ship them over, and the thing is done.
>   Study this art, make it thy great design;
>   And if God's image move thee not, let thine.
>
> (ll. 91-102)

Whatever one thinks of God's, isn't it unnaturally insensitive not to care for one's own image, living in one's child? And, similarly, isn't it absurd, by gambling in the name of pleasure to gain pain? Occasionally the appeal to self-interest is so naked that a reader may misunderstand. When Herbert remarks, 'Think heav'n a better bargain, than to give / Only thy single market-money for it,' he does not mean to imply that *he* thinks salvation is something we can 'purchase,' bargain or not; rather, assuming an audience which responds to prudential arguments, he uses such arguments to emphasize the absurdity of what ordinarily passes for rational behaviour.

In addition to presenting the moral life as the truly rational one, Herbert, like many moralists, comes near to identifying good morals with good manners. He gets to the heart of it: courtesy as the expression of the desire to make things easy for others and to please them—and surely that is congruent with charity, and can form an admirable basis for social behaviour? He is a shrewd and detailed observer. Successful conversation depends upon a variety of experience and a nimble attention to one's audience:

> In thy discourse, if thou desire to please:
> All such is courteous, useful, new, or witty.
> Usefulness comes by labour, wit by ease;
> Courtesy grows in court; news in the city.
>> Get a good stock of these then draw the card
>> That suits him best, of whom thy speech is heard.
>>> (ll. 289-94)

When one argues, he should not become angry:

> Be calm in arguing: for fierceness makes
> Error a fault, and truth discourtesy.
> Why should I feel another man's mistakes
> More than his sicknesses or poverty?
>> In love I should: but anger is not love,
>> Nor wisdom neither: therefore gently move.
>>> (ll. 307-12)

The conversational monopolist is related firmly to the glutton who eats the food of everyone else:

> If thou be master-gunner, spend not all
> That thou canst speak, at once; but husband it,
> And give men turns of speech: do not forestall
> By lavishness thine own, and others' wit,
>> As if thou madst thy will. A civil guest
>> Will no more talk all, than eat all the feast.
>>> (ll. 301-6)

Herbert can also be a subtle casuist, determining carefully the limits of rival moral claims. Renaissance literature is filled with commonplaces about ideal friendship:

the usual exemplars were Damon and Pythias—and Herbert cited David and Jonathan and Christ and John. Herbert was thoroughly traditional when he remarked that 'If cause require' you must be your friend's 'sacrifice.' The usual literary text left it there: the climactic event of the ideal friendship was usually the proof afforded by a man's sacrificing his fortune, his life, or even his lady for the sake of his friend. But Herbert, who took his idealism seriously, went on to point out, hard-headedly, that a married man is no longer free for such an action, since he has no right to sacrifice primary obligations to sentimental allegiances nor to be generous with what does not belong to him; and even the single man has no right to give surety for an amount greater than the value of his estate and personal expectations, since one man cannot justly guarantee to do the work of more than one man.

Along with the sharpness of judgement, the examination of popular assumptions, and the deflation of high-flown sentiments, there is also a marvellous openness, an ability to examine and put to use almost anything at all. Herbert does warn his youth that 'Who follows all things, forfeiteth his will': you really may lose your own mind if you attempt to keep up with every fashion. But yet, without any sense of frenetic search for novelty, one should adopt 'foreign wisdom' rather than simply stick to custom and tradition:

> All foreign wisdom doth amount to this,
> To take all that is given; whether wealth,
> Or love, or language; nothing comes amiss:
> A good digestion turneth all to health.   (ll. 355-58)

The climactic stanzas about public worship are characteristic, in their witty use of proverbial love, their detailed attention to manners as reflections of significant

attitudes, their rhetorical inventiveness, and their lively
rhythms:

> Though private prayer be a brave design,
> Yet public hath more promises, more love:
> And love's a weight to hearts, to eyes a sign.
> We all are but cold suitors; let us move
>   Where it is warmest. Leave thy six and seven;
>   Pray with the most: for where most pray, is heaven.
>
> When once thy foot enters the church, be bare.
> God is more there, than thou: for thou art there
> Only by his permission. Then beware,
> And make thyself all reverence and fear.
>   Kneeling ne'er spoiled silk stockings: quit thy state.
>   All equal are within the church's gate.
>
> Resort to sermons, but to prayers most:
> Praying's the end of preaching. O be drest;
> Stay not for th' other pin: why, thou hast lost
> A joy for it worth worlds. Thus hell doth jest
>   Away thy blessings, and extremely flout thee,
>   Thy clothes being fast, but thy soul loose about thee.
>   (ll. 397-414)

The last two stanzas tell the youth to take a spiritual
inventory each night and to 'play the man.' The final
couplet is Herbert's adaptation of a Stoic epigram:

> If thou do ill; the joy fades, not the pains:
> If well; the pain doth fade, the joy remains.

It is to the point, I think, that the epigram is attributed to
a speech which Cato the Censor gave in 195 B.C.;[14] for
there is a sense in which it and all of 'The Church-
porch' are 'pre-Christian,' despite the poem's assumption
of baptism and church attendance. But Herbert's title
does not merely indicate a place outside the church: the

'Church-porch' should be walked through in order to reach the door of his 'Church.' The rules and lessons, the prudential advice and the admonitory language are necessary, according to the first of the following quatrains labelled 'Superliminare,' as a Perirranterium for sprinkling the holy water of ceremonial cleansing before the youth is admitted to the Church's 'mystical repast.' The second quatrain is in the form of a spell, forbidding the profane or evil reader or spirit from venturing further:

> Avoid, Profaneness; come not heare:
> Nothing but holy, pure, and clear,
> Or that which groaneth to be so,
> May at his peril further go.

The youth who has read and responded to 'The Church-porch' has learned the rudiments of external behaviour, and he has established at least his desire to be holy, pure, and clear. But when he enters 'The Church,' the central section of Herbert's lyrics, he will find that he is in an almost completely different world of thought and discourse. The first thing the reader meets in 'The Church' is the altar of praise to God built of the poet's broken heart—an emblem of the entire volume. The second is the full and sufficient 'Sacrifice' of Christ on the Cross, with Christ Himself as the speaker. In these and the poems which follow, the primary subject is no longer the activities of man but the love of God. Sins are no longer seen as chiefly stupid or self-destructive, but as ungrateful affronts to God's love and Christ's sufferings, or barriers to the understanding and enjoyment of the manifestations of that love. Only rarely does the speaker seem to argue with human critics for specific ideas or observances; rather the 'thou' is usually God. The reader is assumed to identify with that first-person voice, the 'I' or the 'we' which Herbert, like St. Paul, knew was almost inevitable when we attempt to speak either of our innermost experience or the highest Christian mysteries. It is also, of course, the characteristic voice of much of the greatest lyric poetry.

Nothing in 'The Church-porch' truly prepares us for the astonishing variety which follows in 'The Church.' Izaak Walton reported that Herbert told Nicholas Ferrar he could see in the poems 'a picture of the many spiritual conflicts that have past betwixt God and my Soul, before I could subject mine to the will of Jesus my Master: in whose service I have now found perfect freedom.'[15] That death-bed description can mislead any reader who imagines all religious 'spiritual conflicts' in the popular terms of the past century: Is there a God? What is good? What do I believe? Should I or shouldn't I? Am I damned? If these are the defining issues, then most of Herbert's lyrics are hardly 'religious' at all; and they are hardly any more so if we think of the religious as immediately concerned with abstract theological definitions or controversies. (Herbert may have excluded the William's Manuscript's 'The H. Communion' and 'Trinity Sunday' from his final collection of *The Temple* because he thought they went too far in that direction.) Instead of being 'about religion,' the poems are the reflections and creations of a religious life: the hymns, complaints, cries, laments, examinations, quarrels, rejoicings, and promises of a talented poet who was most concerned with the relation of his experience to God's works and Word. If we think of *The Temple* as a picture of 'spiritual conflicts,' we must recognize that such conflicts are almost congruent with human life; that for Herbert they included truces and celebrations and victorious games as well as

97

revolts and wounds and parleys; and that all were a part of the ultimate victory of love.

The poems in 'The Church' range from the most extraordinary simplicity to the most intricate fancifulness. Few other English poets have achieved such powerful effects from monosyllabic lines:

> I struck the board, and cried, 'No more.'
> ('The Collar')
> Sure thou didst put a mind there, if I could
> Find where it lies.   ('Dulness')

> Love is swift of foot;
> Love's a man of war,
> And can shoot,
> And can hit from far.

> Who can scape his bow?
> That which wrought on thee,
> Brought thee low,
> Needs must work on me.   ('Discipline')

> And in this love, more than in bed, I rest ('Evensong')

But equally characteristic is the playfulness of 'The Star,' where the speaker wishes he could join the beams around Christ's face,

> That so among the rest I may
> Glitter and curl, and wind as they:
> That winding is their fashion
> Of adoration.

That 'winding' extends to an anagram, an echo poem ('Heaven'), a hidden acrostic ('Our life is hid with Christ in God'), poems based on the punning interpretation of initals, syllables, and a word ('Love-joy' 'Iesu,' and 'The Sonne'), a 'pruning' poem ('Paradise'), 'A Wreath,' a circular poem ('Sin's Round'), different kinds of 'broken' forms ('Denial' and 'Grief'), the inner transformation of external form in 'Aaron,' the dissolution of form in 'Church monuments,' in addition to the more startling 'pattern poems,' 'The Altar' and 'Easterwings.' Aside from his unusual sonnets, Herbert rarely repeated a form. Whether organized as songs, narratives, questions, dialogues, mediations, 'quips,' or whatever, the poems evidence a metrical virtuosity which makes Herbert the most consistently interesting experimenter in the English lyric between Sidney and Yeats. He explored the possibilities of varying patterns of line lengths and rhymes independently of each other; on the simple *abab* rhyme scheme, for example, he constructed twenty-nine different stanzaic patterns;[16] and using one pattern of line-lengths in 'Man,' he varied the rhyme scheme to form an image of the providential variety of man's gifts and abilities and relationships.[17] Herbert devoted his 'utmost art' to the making of his poems, whether he concealed it with conscious simplicity or displayed it openly and with delight.

The poems within 'The Church' will repay almost any amount of study we wish to devote to them. It is they, of course, which establish Herbert's stature as a poet. I think we may read them better if, by means of an attentive reading of 'The Church-porch,' we have come to realize how firmly Herbert's worship and self-examination were grounded in the ordinary events of daily life and a concern for the selves of others. He is the least solipsistic of poets. 'The Church-porch' demonstrates Herbert's knowledge of the fact that moral persuasion is likely to be most effective when a speaker addresses an audience in its own language concerning its own problems, with a demonstrated concern for its essential good and happiness.

Perhaps the poem may have served Herbert as a way of establishing the nature of the reader he assumed 'over his shoulder,' as well as of purging the immediate didactic impulse which sometimes haunts any conscientious user of language. He may then have been able to turn more freely in the other poems to other uses of language in the service of poetry and the worship of God.

But mastery of rhetorical persuasion such as 'The Church-porch' demonstrates was in no way antithetical to the creation of the highest 'personal' poetry. Rhetorical mastery for a seventeenth-century poet implied merely that he had learned a good deal about how language works and had developed an ability to relate efficiently his verbal means and ends. Like other skills and powers, it could, of course, be dangerous. But its chief dangers, triviality, bullying, and pomposity, were not serious ones for a man who wrote clearly neither from vanity nor for power but out of love.

Herbert placed as the last poem within 'The Church,' after the poems on 'Death,' 'Doomsday,' 'Judgement,' and 'Heaven,' the four last things, the third poem to which he gave the title 'Love.' That poem is an imaginative description of the first reception of the soul into the heavenly communion, of which the earthly eucharist is but a foretaste. It is a very moving poem, and it derives a large part of its power from the very simplicity of its means. That overpowering meeting, face to face with Incarnate Love, is told as the simplest narrative and dialogue of the most ordinary kind: a traveller, conscious of his unworthiness, is reluctant to be a guest; but his scruples are overcome by the kindest and most courteous of hosts:

> Love bade me welcome: yet my soul drew back,
> Guilty of dust and sin.

But quick-eyed Love, observing me grow slack
    From my first entrance in,
Drew nearer to me, sweetly questioning,
    If I lacked any thing.

'A guest,' I answered, 'worthy to be here:'
    Love said, 'You shall be he.'
'I the unkind, ungrateful? Ah my dear,
    I cannot look on thee.'
Love took my hand, and smiling did reply,
    'Who made the eyes but I?'

'Truth Lord, but I have marred them: let my shame
    God where it doth deserve.'
'And know you not,' says Love, 'Who bore the blame?'
    'My dear, then I will serve.'
'You must sit down,' says Love, 'and taste my meat:'
    So I did sit and eat.

What Herbert learned about rhetoric and Christian persuasion is evident in 'Love.'

CHAPTER IV

A Foreign and a Provincial Gentleman:
Richard Crashaw and Henry Vaughan

RICHARD CRASHAW, the son of an eminent
Puritan clergyman, was twenty years younger than
Herrick, Carew, King and George Herbert, and
the exact contemporary of that best-selling poet John
Cleveland. His *Epigrammatum Sacrorum Liber*, the only
volume that he saw through the press, was published in
1634, the year after *The Temple*. His first volume con-
taining English poems did not appear until 1646, after
Crashaw, a recent convert to Rome, had left England for
Paris. The preface to that volume,[1] probably written by
Crashaw's friend and contemporary Joseph Beaumont,[2]
explains the title given to the English sacred poems:
'Reader, we style his Sacred Poems, *Steps to the Temple*,
and aptly, for in the Temple of God, under his wing, he
led his life in St. *Mary's* Church near St. *Peter's* College . . .
There, he penned these Poems, *Steps* for happy souls to
climb heaven by.' Although Crashaw had indeed been a
Fellow at Peterhouse, Cambridge, the explanation seems
a little disingenuous. Surely the more likely reason for
the title (probably provided either by Beaumont or the
publisher rather than the poet) is suggested earlier in the
Preface: 'Here's *Herbert's* second, but equal, who hath
retrieved poetry of late, and returned it up to its primitive
use; Let it bound back to heaven gates, whence it came.'
The Temple had been remarkably popular. Christopher
Harvey had published *The Synagogue: Or, The Shadow of
The Temple* (including within it 'A Stepping Stone to the

Nimia,
second
owe a

ʒdalene
differ-
esents a
ational

ts.

lene,

rbert's Church-Porch') as early as
Herbert's volume had already gone
editions. To present a friend's new
verse under a title related to *The*
attempt to attract a wide and ready

ps to the Temple* makes almost equally
wledge of Herbert's volume and his
e of its influence:

Herbert's booke intituled the Temple of
Poems, sent to a Gentlewoman.

Fair on what you look?
ve lies in this book:
îre from your eyes,
this his sacrifice.
r hand unties these strings,
l've an Angel by the wings.
gladly will be nigh
pon each morning sigh,
in the balmy air,
vell perfumèd prayer.
lite plumes of his he'll lend you,
ery day to heaven will send you:
acquaintance of the sphere,
he smooth faced kindred there.
ugh *Herbert's* name do owe
evotions, fairest; know
nile I lay them on the shrine
white hand, they are mine.

of gallant compliment and decorative
all like Herbert: there are no flutterings
'well-perfumèd prayers' in *The Temple*.
e of seven- and eight-syllable couplets is
bert's verse. As Austin Warren pointed

out,[3] only one of Crashaw's poems, 'Charitas
or The Dear Bargain' (not published until the
edition of *Steps to the Temple* in 1648) seems t
substantial debt to Herbert.

The two poets' poetic treatments of St. Mary M:
demonstrate in a dramatic fashion their essentia
ences. Herbert's poem is fully characteristic: it pl
situation, questions its significance, and suggests a
(and also a touching) solution:

> When blessed Mary wiped her Saviour's feet
> (Whose precepts she had trampled on before),
> And wore them for a jewel on her head,
>   Showing his steps should be the street,
>   Wherein she thenceforth evermore
> With pensive humbleness would live and tread:
>
> She being stained herself, why did she strive
> To make him clean, who could not be defiled?
> Why kept she not her tears for her own faults,
>   And not his feet? Though we could dive
>   In tears like seas, our sins are piled
> Deeper than they, in words, and works, and thoug
>
> Dear soul, she knew who did vouchsafe and deign
> To bear her filth; and that her sins did dash
> Ev'n God himself: wherefore she was not loth,
>   As she had brought wherewith to stain,
>   So to bring in wherewith to wash:
> And yet in washing one, she washèd both.

Crashaw's poem is the notorious 'Saint Mary Magc
or The Weeper,' which begins,

> Hail, *Sister Springs*,
> Parents of silver-forded rills!
> Ever bubbling things!
> *Thawing Christal! Snowy Hills!*

> Still spending, never spent; I mean
> Thy fair Eyes sweet *Magdalene*.

Austin Warren has described the poem as 'a free fantasia':
'From his poem Crashaw has excluded the story, the
character, the psychology, and the moral. Mary has no
part in her poem; it should be called not "The Weeper"
but "Tears" . . . It is a theme with variations—only the
variations lack much variety: they do not change timbre
or increase in resonance; and though they are all ingenious
even their ingenuity is not climactic.'[4] If Crashaw took
the phrase 'crystal viols' from Donne,[5] it is surely all that
the poem owes to him. And with this poem, in contrast to
the little poem on sending *The Temple* to a 'gentlewoman,'
one can hardly imagine a debt to Jonson or even the minor
Jonsonians. Although there are lines and phrases that
remind one of Spenser or the Spenserians, the chief
literary indebtednesses here are, for an English poet of the
time, more unusual: to the Jesuit Latin poets, Francis
Remond, Baudouin Cabilliau of Ypres, and Herman
Hugo, and particularly to that poet of the astounding,
Giambattista Marino. If William Drummond of Haw-
thornden, who had to listen to Ben Jonson tell him that his
verses were old-fashioned, read Crashaw's book and still
cared about such things, he must have taken some satis-
faction in seeing a brilliantly 'new' young poet turn from
the once-fashionable Donne and the dictatorial Jonson to
one of the Italian poets Drummond had admired and
translated.

Crashaw became the chief English poet of the Counter
Reformation. His poems do not usually invite us primarily
to rational understanding or even the appreciation of a
performance, but to rapt participation in ecstatic joys and
sufferings or delight in decorative and sensuous ornament.

We are not expected to *judge* such poetry but to identify with its emotional states, to become entranced by its mellifluous sounds, to be shocked delightfully by its conceits and its occasionally outrageous epithets. Douglas Bush has suggested that 'poetry like Crashaw's' may serve as the simplest definition of what most people mean when they talk about 'baroque poetry'; he also remarked that its motto might be, 'Over-ripeness is all.'[6] This is the Crashaw who is called 'un-English,' sometimes with the tone of shocked propriety appropriate to an occasion when a child with the wrong blood lines inherits a valuable familial estate—or even with the moral indignation which often accompanies the phrase, 'un-American.'

Crashaw is unusual, and he does present problems for both the critics and the literary historians. I think that one can identify the responses of two partisan groups, both of which strike me as mistaken: those who do not much like Crashaw's poetry and tend to attribute what they consider its failings to ignorance (he didn't know what he was doing), or to incompetence (he couldn't do anything else), or to his corruption by the Italians and Roman Catholics; and those who are such ardent defenders that they admit no shortcomings whatsoever and claim that he was always in control of his forms and images, that his language was never unusually sensual or sexual, and that any impression to the contrary is only the result of our incompetence in reading and responding to traditional religious symbolic language. Those extremes tend to obscure not only some of the radical problems but also some of the unusual possibilities of Crashaw's poetry.

Since one can glimpse most of the problems within *The Delights of the Muses*, the separately titled secular poems which were printed along with *Steps to the Temple* in both 1646 and 1648, I think it is best to begin there, undistracted by the special and complicated issues raised by the religious verse. One poem in that collection, 'Upon two green Apricocks sent to *Cowley* by Sir *Crashaw*,' probably written when he was in his early twenties, shows that Crashaw could, when he wished, achieve impressive mastery of the sort of ingenious, witty, tightly-organized seventeenth-century poem so admired in the first half of the twentieth century. Cowley had published his *Poetical Blossoms* in 1633, when he was only fifteen years old. (Three years later he dared to apologize for the immaturity of one of the poems on the grounds that it had been written when he was only ten.) Crashaw was five years older than Cowley, already a fellow at Peterhouse when Cowley went up to Trinity. Crashaw turned his two green apricots into a graceful comment on his own late poetic immaturity in comparison to Cowley's astonishingly early fruits and flowers:

> O had my wishes
> And the dear merits of your Muse, their due,
> The year had found some fruit early as you;
> Ripe as those rich composures time computes
> Blossoms, but our blest taste confesses fruits.
>
> (ll. 10-14)

The poem ends with lines of elegance and power that go quite beyond conventional compliment:

> How then must these,
> Poor fruits look pale at thy Hesperides!
> Fain would I chide their slowness, but in their
> Defects I draw mine own dull character.
> Take them, and me in them acknowledging,
> How much my summer waits upon thy spring.
>
> (ll. 29-34)

If anyone wishes further evidence of Crashaw's abilities in this direction, he can find it, again in relation to Cowley, in the poem 'On Hope,' printed among the sacred poems in *Steps to the Temple*. There, in alternate stanzas, Cowley attacked the hope that appears in the guises of worldly anticipation, greed, and coxcombry, and Crashaw defended the theological virtue that goes under the same name. In that poem Crashaw equalled Cowley in wit and neatness and far surpassed him in warmth and imaginative range. The final couplet is one of Crashaw's finest:

> True *Hope's* a glorious Huntress, and her chase
> The God of Nature in the field of Grace.

Wit and economy were of the essence in most of the Latin epigrams. If Crashaw did not write more poems like these it was because he preferred to write another kind of poetry.

One finds other and stranger things in *The Delights of the Muses*. The author of those poems shared much of the typical seventeenth-century young man's interest in decorative amatory poetry. (In addition to Marino and some of the Italian madrigalists, Crashaw used the fairly standard classical texts: Moschus's 'Cupid's Crier,' Ausonius, Catullus's 'Seize the Day' once again.) One of the more memorable couplets in this vein is from the epigram 'Upon *Venus* putting on *Mars* his Arms':

> Mars thou hast beaten naked, and o then
> What need'st thou put on arms against poor men?

But if almost anyone might have tried his hand at adapting another epigram from the Greek Anthology (although seldom with such neatness), I think there is a good deal more than the usual literary taste and sensual suscepti-

bility in Crashaw's translation of a passage from Virgil's
Georgics,[7] 'In the praise of the Spring':

> All trees, all leavy groves confess the Spring
> Their gentlest friend, then, then the lands begin
> To swell with forward pride, and seed desire
> To generation; Heaven's Almighty Sire
> Melts on the bosom of his love, and pours
> Himself into her lap in fruitful showers.
> And by a soft insinuation, mixt
> With earth's large mass, doth cherish and assist
> Her weak conceptions; No lone shade, but rings
> With chatting birds' delicious murmurings.
> Then *Venus'* mild instinct (at set times) yields
> The herds to kindly meetings, then the fields
> (Quick with warm *Zephyr's* lively breath) lay forth
> Their pregnant bosoms in a fragrant birth.
> Each body's plump and juicy, all things full
> Of supple moisture. . . .   (ll. 1-16)

The rhythms of those fervent, astonishingly enjambed
lines, are not those associated with witty point; they
anticipate some of Milton's. I think it most unlikely that
the young man who wrote those lines would ever make
unconscious or unintentional use of a large amount of
sexual imagery or allusion.

In the forty-two triplets of 'Wishes. To his (supposed)
Mistress' (the poem that begins: 'Who e'er she be, / That
not impossible she / That shall command my heart and
me') one can see another of Crashaw's individual qualities: his tendency towards copious, almost infinite,
variations. A version of that poem containing only ten
triplets was published earlier, in the second edition of
Wits Recreations (1641); it has a clearer shape than the
1646-1648 version and it is nearer to what we ordinarily
think of as 'a poem' (even, perhaps, a 'Jonsonian' poem),

but it is less interesting and much less a characteristic poem by Crashaw. Reading the full version, one can imagine that, as with the first version of 'The Weeper,' still more additional stanzas could have been added or these stanzas rearranged with very little harm—or improvement—to the poem. Related to the multiplication of variations is Crashaw's tendency to expand greatly his models or originals. That is clear enough in 'Music's Duel,' the poem about a contest between a nightingale and a lutanist, where Crashaw turned Famianus Strada's 58 Latin lines into 168 English ones, expanding the 14-line description of the actual 'duel' to 100 lines. That poem also demonstrates Crashaw's fascination with the emotional effects of sounds, and his agility (and delight) in moving rapidly from one image or sensory response to another, mixing or confusing them to the point that, while the mind can sometimes hardly disentangle the 'prose meanings' (which often seem to cancel each other), the lines powerfully suggest an ardent voice, excess, and ecstasy:[8]

> Then starts she suddenly into a throng
> Of short thick sobs, whose thund'ring volleys float,
> And roll themselves over her lubric throat
> In panting murmurs, 'stilled out of her breast
> That ever-bubbling spring; the sugared Nest
> Of her delicious soul, that there does lie
> Bathing in streams of liquid Melody;
> Music's best seed-plot, whence in ripened Aires
> A golden-headed harvest, fairly rears
> His honey-dropping tops, plowed by her breath
> Which there reciprocally laboureth
> In that sweet soil.   (ll. 62-73)

There was a time when I confidently judged effects such as those in 'Wishes to his (supposed) Mistress' and

'Music's Duel' to be somehow illegitimate, but I now attribute my prejudiced response to youthful conservatism Why, after all, should there not be a poetry of excess as well as ecstasy? Why should we tie everything to logical or rhetorical schemata or notions of necessarily obvious beginnings and middles and ends? What is wrong with the idea of an open-ended form? As the American poet Elizabeth Bishop once casually remarked, why shouldn't Western poetry, like Eastern music, explore the possibilities of theoretically infinite variations? (Of course eventually we would get tired; and then the poem might stop or we might, individually, stop reading it.) Such questions are likely to disturb our few, hard-won concepts concerning a coherent poetics, and they may prove particularly upsetting if we have tried to make literature into a surrogate for religion. But we should try not to be afraid of unusual ideas, and it is just such possibilities that Crashaw's poetry suggests. If we read 'Wishes to his (supposed) Mistress' with such queries in mind rather than with the assumption that the poem intends (or should intend) to 'build' and fails to do so, we may find that we enjoy nearly all of those occasionally repetitious triplets, and we may come to question the assumption that every poem should be 'built' as if it were a house. There are other things that we can do with poems besides try to live within them, and there are other possible constructions besides houses—or even temples. As Crashaw remarked in some of his finest lines, 'The phoenix builds the phoenix' nest. / Love's architecture is his own.'[9]

From the secular poems it seems obvious that by temperament and desire Crashaw was early destined to be an unusual kind of English poet. He was fortunate, I think, to find in the Italian Jesuit poets and in the

Catholicism of the Counter Reformation sustaining traditions, guides, and perhaps restraints. His religious poems present more problems for the modern reader— and many more rewards. It is within them that Crashaw developed most fully both his voice of exclamatory apostrophe (whether addressed to an absent lady, a book, a saint, or the name of Jesus) and his dithyrambic movements of mixed meters (suggesting the suddenly shifting movements characteristic of intense emotion) which Cowley was to popularize as the 'English' or 'irregular' Pindaric ode. Crashaw is not always surely in control. He falters, I think, when he concentrates on one desired meaning or effect so intensely that he fails to anticipate (and prevent) the possibility of a disastrous secondary one. That seems to be the problem when in 'The Weeper' he means to emphasize the relations between the precious, nourishing tears and the angelic music, but unfortunately says that the angel's song 'Tastes of this breakfast all day long'; and also when he means to relate the precious essence of roses to the fires of its distilling process, but mistakenly describes the rose as 'Sweating in a too warm bed.' But I think Crashaw knew exactly what he was doing and was fully in control in 'On a prayer book sent to Mrs. M. R.,' a poem that ends with the lines,

> Happy soul, she shall discover,
>   What joy, what bliss,
>   How many heavens at once it is,
> To have a God become her lover.

Crashaw clearly intended there, as elsewhere, to devote the language of sexual love to the higher spiritual ecstasy, and it is no accident that, as Bush has noted,[10] one can find in that poem a number of the same images that one finds in

Carew's erotic masterpiece, 'The Rapture.' No one can make us like such effects, of course, but we have no right to avoid the issue either by claiming that the mystical tradition had eliminated in advance all the sexual implications of Crashaw's language, or by assuming that the effects are the result of an inadvertent slipping of the poet's ordinary mask from his unconscious. Crashaw's strain of love is at its best, I think, in the St. Teresa poems. 'A Hymn to the Name and Honor of the Admirable Saint Teresa' is consciously controlled and carefully revised, and it is an astonishing poem.

I cannot read Crashaw every day, and I cannot ordinarily read many of his poems at a sitting. Some of the poems which my friends admire seem to me to go on a good deal longer than they need to. (Occasionally, however, and with other works besides Crashaw's, I find it useful to remind myself of Stephen Crane's judgement on *War and Peace*: it was too long.) When for whatever reason one discovers that he cannot share at all in the excitement, Crashaw's rhapsodies can seem both tedious and tasteless. It may be a mark of my generally conservative taste that the poem which strikes me as most fully successful as a whole should be 'An Hymn of the Nativity, sung by the Shepherds,' where the traditional materials and the formal divisions between two shepherds and the chorus provide an obvious and firm structure for the poem. At any rate, it is a lovely poem, and one of those which Crashaw carefully improved by his revisions. Its most dramatic moment (in the 1648 version) occurs when, after Thyrsis and Tityris have joined together in the repetition of an earlier stanza celebrating their sight of the Child, the full chorus repeats the stanza once again and goes on to the magnificent beginning of their welcome to Him and all the paradoxes that He represents.

BOTH

We saw thee in thy balmy nest
    Bright *Dawn* of our eternal *Day*,
We saw thine eyes break from their *East*
    And chase the trembling shades away
We saw thee, and we blest the sight,
We saw thee, by thine own sweet light.

CHORUS

We saw thee, and we blest the sight,
We saw thee, by thine own sweet light.

FULL CHORUS

Welcome, all *wonders* in one sight!
    Eternity shut in a span,
Summer in winter, day in night,
    Heaven in earth, and God in man;
Great little one! whose all embracing birth
Lifts earth to heav'n, stoops heav'n to earth.

Fine as those stanzas are, though, I do not think they are quite Crashaw's greatest lines. I would judge those to be the concluding lines of 'The Flaming Heart: Upon the Book and Picture of the seraphical Saint Teresa (as she is usually expressed with a Seraphim beside her)' lines which appeared only in the *Carmen Deo Nostro* version of the poem, published in 1652 after Crashaw's death in Loreto. Within them, I think that Crashaw most successfully transformed the hyperboles and ardours of ordinary lovers' language into a triumphantly new language for a new and supreme love. The lines may remind us in some respects of Blake. Neither Blake nor any other English poet has ever been able to sustain for long such incandescence:

O thou undaunted daughter of desires!
By all thy dower of *Lights* and *Fires*;
By all the eagle in thee, all the dove;
By all thy lives and deaths of love;
By thy large draughts of intellectual day,
And by thy thirsts of love more large than they;
By all thy brim-fill'd Bowles of fierce desire;
By thy last morning's draught of liquid fire;
By the full kingdom of that final kiss
That seiz'd thy parting soul, and seal'd thee his;
By all the heav'ns thou hast in him
(Fair sister of the Seraphim!)
By all of *Him* we have in *Thee*;
Leave nothing of my *Self* in me.
Let me so read thy life, that I
Unto all life of mine may die.

If Crashaw found in Italy sustenance for a sort of poetry which was, in its intensity and accomplishment, new to England, Henry Vaughan did not have to go farther than Wales to depart almost as far from the central English literary traditions of his time and to be equally successful as an innovator—perhaps it might be more accurately said that he hardly left Wales.[11] Born in Brecknockshire about ten years after Crashaw's birth, Vaughan seems to have gone, along with his twin brother Thomas, to Jesus College, that centre of Welsh culture in Oxford. Henry stayed only about two years (probably from his sixteenth to eighteenth years) and then studied law for another two years in London. But he took no degrees, and by the beginning of the civil war (in which he saw active service) he was back in Brecknock, in Brecon or Newton, where he later practised medicine for many years. (We know nothing of any medical training.) During his long life he hardly seems to have left his shire again.

One gets some touching glimpses of the young Henry Vaughan from his *Poems, With the Tenth Satire of Juvenal Englished*, which he published in 1646, the same year as Crashaw's *Steps to the Temple*. In a self-conscious prefatory letter 'To all Ingenious Lovers of Poesy,'[12] Vaughan insisted on his genteel casualness, his distance from the 'dull Times,' his publication only for kindred 'refined Spirits,' and also on the 'Innocence' of his 'flame' ('the fire at highest is but Platonic'). That letter, like the entire volume, has the air of being hopefully sent from the provinces to an unknown and almost unimaginable audience. The poems which follow show a young man in his early twenties trying hard to be a poet and very busy imitating fashionable poets and attitudes. In the opening poem, Vaughan put Ben Jonson first in the 'Elysium' of poets (with Thomas Randolph as his only individually mentioned fellow), and in a number of poems he showed that he had read his Donne:

> 'Tis true, I am undone; Yet e'er I die,
> I'll leave these sighs, and tears a legacy
> To after-lovers. . . .   ('An Elegy')

> (Though fate, and time each day remove
> Those things that element their love)
>   ('To Amoret gone from him')

> Just so base, sublunary lovers' hearts
>   Fed on loose profane desires,
>   May for an eye,
>   Or face comply:
> But those removed, they will as soon depart,

And show their art,
And painted fires.

('To Amoret, of the
difference 'twixt him, and other
Lovers, and what true Love is')

Some of the Donne and Jonson echoes may have been
reinforced or filtered through the example of William
Habington, another imitator of both Donne and Jonson,
and a Worcestershire man who had married Lucy Herbert
daughter of Lord Powys. (Much of the second- as well as
first-rate lyric poetry of the century was Welsh or West
Country either in its origins or associations.) One can also
see Vaughan's alarming tendency to appropriate almost
verbatim several lines together from Owen Felltham's
Resolves. But none of it really seems promising. Vaughan
can occasionally write effective lines, but most of the time
he is uncertainly attempting an unconvincing tone. His
try at tavern verse and 'merry, mad mirth' in 'A Rhap-
sody' is simply not very merry and not at all mad. The
author of that poem seems to attempt a roguish role for
which he is qualified neither by temperament nor by
experience. As when an older man tries too hard to keep
up with a younger crowd, one wishes he wouldn't.

Olor Iscanus, 'The Swan of Usk,' which Vaughan
prepared for publication in 1647, shows some advances,
particularly in one of its verse letters ('To his retired
friend, an Invitation to Brecknock') and in 'An Elegy on
the death of Mr. R. W. slain in the late unfortunate
differences at Rowton Heath, near Chester, 1645,' but
most of the volume is hardly more promising. In addition
to more elegies and verse letters, some Latin epigrams,
translations of Ovid (from *Tristia* and *Ex Ponto* only),
Boethius, and 'the divine Casimir' (the Polish Jesuit

117

Sarbiewski, whose Latin odes had such a vogue), there are numerous examples of the saddest of all seventeenth-century genres: commendatory poems which the writers or publishers of the works praised never even put to their obvious uses as prefatory puffing. In this category are the poems praising Gombauld's *Endymion*, Fletcher's plays, the poems of Katherine Philips ('The Matchless Orinda'), and Davenant's *Gondibert.* Vaughan's poem praising William Cartwright's poems and plays at least was published in its destined place in Cartwright's volume; and the one on Thomas Powell's translation of Malvezzi's *Christian Politician* would surely have been reprinted had Powell's work ever achieved publication. Two of Henry Vaughan's friends who had been at Oxford offered commendatory poems for his own volume, and Thomas Vaughan, the alchemical twin, provided another, in which he insisted too much that they *could* have got more puffs had they really tried. The title-page's tag from Virgil's *Georgics, Flumina amo, Sylvasque inglorius,* also seems to protest too much on the poet's proud lack of fame. *Olor Iscanus* would leave us with a most pathetic impression except for the fact that by the time Vaughan's anonymous friend published it in 1651, the first part of *Silex Scintillans* had already appeared; and the poet who could write that volume need hardly be pitied or patronized by any reader of English poetry.

The two parts of *Silex Scintillans* (1650, 1655) are even more inexplicable than the usual appearances of poetic genius. After writing two undistinguished volumes of verse, a provincial poetaster about twenty-six years of age suddenly began (probably in 1648) to write religious poetry, much of it of the highest quality, and he composed over one-hundred and thirty poems within a seven year period. Then no more poetry appeared for twenty-three years. *Thalia Rediviva: The Pass-Times and Diversions of a Country-Muse* was published in 1678. It contained more secular poems resembling the uninteresting earlier ones, more translations, and a few religious poems which reflect some of the sudden glory but which certainly do not add anything to Vaughan's poetic stature. Five years before that last volume, in 1673, Vaughan was writing his cousin John Aubrey, listing his own and his brother's publications, giving information about Welsh Oxford men, and again assuming the outsider's tone: 'I am highly obliged to you that you would be pleased to remember, and reflect upon such low and forgotten things, as my brother and myself.'[13] Sixteen years later, in 1689, he remarked a bit sharply to Anthony Wood, 'If you intend a second edition of the Oxford-history, I must give you a better account of my brothers' books and mine; which are in the first much mistaken, and many omitted.'[14] But it seems almost too symbolic that on October 9, 1694, when he was seventy-two or seventy-three, Vaughan should have given, in reply to Aubrey's inquiry about Welsh bards, a circumstantial account of a young Welsh shepherd's bardic seizure:

> This vein of poetry they called Awen, which in their language signifies as much as Raptus, or a poetic furor; and (in truth) as many of them as I have conversed with are (as I may say) gifted or inspired with it. I was told by a very sober and knowing person (now dead) that in his time, there was a young lad father and motherless, and so very poor that he was forced to beg; but at last was taken up by a rich man, that kept a great stock of sheep upon the mountains not far from the place where I now dwell, who clothed him and sent him into the mountains to keep his sheep. There in summer time following the sheep and looking to their lambs, he fell into a deep sleep; In which he dreamt, that he saw a beautiful young man with a garland of green leafs upon

his head, and a hawk upon his fist: with a quiver full of arrows at his back, coming towards him (whistling several measures or tunes all the way), and at last let the hawk fly at him, which (he dreamt) got into his mouth and inward parts, and suddenly awaked in a great fear and consternation: but possessed with such a vein, or gift of poetry, that he left his sheep and went about the country, making songs upon all occasions, and came to be the most famous bard in all the country in his time.[15]

Vaughan's seven marvellous years were a prime example of an inspiration that departed as mysteriously as it came. 'The wind bloweth where it listeth,' St. John remarked in a passage Vaughan recalled in his poem 'Regeneration.' And when Vaughan was subject to that inspiration it was not that he had at last mastered the conventional poetic techniques of his time and learned to do well what the others were doing; it seemed rather that, like Ben Jonson's Henry Morison for a while at least,

> He leaped the present age,
> Possessed with holy rage,
> To see that bright eternal day. . . .

Vaughan got his title, *Silex Scintillans*, from a passage of the Jesuit John Nieremberg, which he translated, 'Certain Divine Rays break out of the Soul in adversity, like sparks of fire out of the afflicted *flint*.'[16] Some of the afflictions associated with the sparks and rays that gave rise to the poems are the civil war (Vaughan's poems 'The Constellation' and 'Abel's Blood' are two of the century's most impressive poems which deal directly with that conflict), the death of his younger brother, and later, his own illness and the death of his wife. But in his preface to the second part of *Silex Scintillans*, after having lamented his and other wits' former 'deliberate search, or excogitation of *idle words*, and a most vain, insatiable desire to be reputed *Poets*,' Vaughan showed that he considered his new devotion to religious verse directly attributable to one earthly agent:

> The first, that with any effectual success attempted a diversion of this foul and overflowing stream, was the blessed man, Mr. George Herbert, whose holy life and verse gained many pious Converts, (of whom I am the least). . . .[17]

That statement should prove no surprise to anyone who has read the poems carefully. As F. E. Hutchinson remarked, no other English poet of any significance ever took so much from another as Vaughan did from Herbert.[18] He took titles, words, phrases, lines, and stanza forms, as well as central themes and subjects. He seems to have known *The Temple* (like the Bible) so well that his borrowings often are unconscious recollections, with Herbert's words or images put to surprisingly different uses or applications. And yet, while it seems that Vaughan might never have been an interesting poet at all without Herbert's inspiration and example, at his best he is quite unlike Herbert. He does not possess Herbert's sense of neatness and order: his poems are often long and sometimes almost shapeless. The complex stanza forms which Herbert invented and used with such precision often seem merely burdens to Vaughan. (On a number of occasions he began a poem with such a stanza and then, after a bit, simply abandoned it for couplets.) At his best Vaughan is not a poet of rational examination, careful craftsmanship, and technical experimentation in the tradition of Sidney and Herbert but a poet of astounding, if erratic, visionary and aural powers. In the first poem within *Silex Scintillans* what immediately strikes most contemporary readers today is not at all the influence of

George Herbert but the clear anticipation of the bardic
voice of Dylan Thomas:

> A ward, and still in bonds, one day
> I stole abroad,
> It was high-spring, and all the way
> *Primrosed*, and hung with shade;
> Yet was it frost within,
> And surly winds
> Blasted my infant buds, and sin
> Like clouds eclipsed my mind.
>
> ('Regeneration')

Vaughan's inspiration, his unselfconsciousness, and
his provinciality proved the sources of his outstanding
strengths as well as weaknesses. I do not think he set out
to write a new sort of poetry any more than he intended
any novel religious emphases.[19] His conscious creedal
formulations were blamelessly othodox (he felt no conflict
between the Bible, the English Prayer Book, and the
hermetic books he read and translated), and poetically he
meant to imitate George Herbert. But anyone in the seventeenth century who responded as intensely as Vaughan
to visions of infant innocence and the beauties of the
Welsh countryside almost inevitably *sounded* novel, both
religiously and poetically. (Reading Vaughan's verse
makes one realize, incidentally, how little in the way of
natural description there is in either Donne or Herbert
or, except for a few poems, in Jonson.) And anyone who
depended so much upon immediate personal inspiration
as Vaughan would almost inevitably have difficulties in
constructing or conveying large systems of thought or
sound. It is difficult to imagine that an English poet who had
attended Westminster School or had been resident longer
or nearer to the universities and the Court and London

would have settled for so many oddly unrhymed lines, lines so twisted to achieve their rhymes, such imperfect rhymes, such awkward shifts in stanzaic and rhetorical constructions, so many sudden (and sometimes even bathetic) poetic descents. But neither was any other English poet capable of writing the stanza I have just quoted, and none began a poem at a height so dizzying as that where Vaughan began 'The World':

> I saw Eternity the other night
> Like a great *Ring* of pure and endless light,
>   All calm, as it was bright,
> And round beneath it, Time in hours, days, years
>   Driv'n by the spheres
> Like a vast shadow moved, in which the world
> And all her train were hurled;. . . .

Immediately thereafter the poem descends with a thud, never to recover, in its description of the world's train. (A borrowing from Herbert's witty poem 'Dulness' marks the descent—the obvious uses of Herbert often seem to mark the places where Vaughan's inspiration failed him.) But instead of spending much time in regretting the fall, we should read and rejoice in the magnificent lines that we are granted.

Such lines often owe at least part of their strange power to odd and what seem to be unidiomatic uses of English. In 'Regeneration,' for example, there is a magic stanza in which the narrator describes the 'new spring' that 'Did all my senses greet':

> The unthrift Sun shot vital gold
>   A thousand pieces,
> And heaven its azure did unfold
>   Checquered with snowy fleeces,

The air was all in spice
And every bush
A garland wore; Thus fed my Eyes
But all the Ear lay hush.   (ll. 41-48)

I think it just possible that an English poet closer to the
ordinary traditions might have attempted the complex,
effective, and triply-mixed metaphor of the sun as an
unthrift with gold pieces, but shooting them like bullets
rather than scattering them like coins, and midway, having them transformed into a 'vital' rather than either a
metallic or a deadly gold. But I do not believe that a more
centrally 'English' poet of the period would have used
what seems the bold coinage of 'The air was all in spice'
(by analogy, I believe, with the bush's being 'in flower')
or would have allowed that odd, dramatic use of 'hush,'
where the verb '*lay*' would seem to require 'hushed'
rather than that archaic adjectival form, 'hush.' ('But all
the Ear lay hush'). I am reminded of a remark of T. S.
Eliot's about the possibilities of dislocating language into
new meanings: that seems to describe accurately what
Vaughan has done. His relative isolation and distance
from a critical audience of conventionally knowing poetic
craftsmen was probably one of the factors which allowed
him the freedom for his new creations. (On the poem
'Regeneration,' I wish to add only that, rather than being
a mysterious description of the precise stages of mystical
vision, I think it more likely to be simply a description of
the speaker's pilgrimage in search both of personal regeneration and also of some rational understanding of the
mysteries concerning that doctrine so crucial to the contemporary arguments on predestination and the freedom
of the will.)

Vaughan's great themes are of innocence and nature,

light and greenness, heavenly and human and even vegetative glory. (F. E. Hutchinson's note that in Welsh the same word serves for *white, fair,* and *blessed*[20] provides a valuable clue to Vaughan's English vocabulary.) Some of the most magnificent passages occur when one sort of glory is seen together with—or in terms of—another or others:

> Man of old
> Within the line
> Of *Eden* could
> Like the Sun shine
> All naked, innocent and bright,
> And intimate with Heav'n, as light.
> > ('Ascension-Hymn,' ll. 19-24)

> Happy those early days! when I
> Shin'd in my Angel-infancy.
> Before I understood this place
> Appointed for my second race,
> Or taught my soul to fancy ought
> But a white, celestial thought,
> When yet I had not walkt above
> A mile, or two, from my first love,
> And looking back (at that short space),
> Could see a glimpse of his bright-face;
> When on some *gilded cloud* or *flower*
> My gazing soul would dwell an hour,
> And in those weaker glories spy
> Some shadows of eternity;
> Before I taught my tongue to wound
> My conscience with a sinful sound,
> Or had the black art to dispense
> A sev'ral sin to ev'ry sense,
> But felt through all this fleshly dress
> Bright *shoots* of everlastingness.
> > ('The Retreat,' ll. 1-20)

O Joys! Infinite sweetness! with what flowers,
And shoots of glory, my soul breaks, and buds!
All the long hours
Of night, and rest
Through the still shrouds
Of sleep, and clouds
This Dew fell on my breast;
O how it *Bloods*
And *Spirits* all my Earth! hark! In what Rings
And *Hymning Circulations* the quick world
Awakes, and sings;
The rising winds,
And falling springs,
Birds, beasts, all things
Adore him in their kinds.
Thus all is hurled
In sacred *Hymns*, and *Order*, The great *Chime*
And *Symphony* of nature.   ('The Morning-watch,'
ll. 1-18)

In some of the poems that are most successful as wholes, such as 'The Night' and 'They are all gone into the world of light!' Vaughan developed a loosely associative structure which is very different from the tightly logical or pseudo-logical structures of Donne and from the neat and carefully articulated structures of Jonson and Herbert. Often framed by a meditation—or a vision—and a prayer, the central section represents various movements of a mind, and the logical or associative connections between those movements are usually not stated but must be intuited by the reader. 'They are all gone into the world of light!' for example, begins with three stanzas that describe the vision and the speaker's situation; then there is a stanza's apostrophe to hope and humility; another apostrophe to Death; an exemplum of the 'fledged bird's nest' with the negative argument of the 'peeps' into man's glory; the analogy of the star in the tomb, with its application clearly implied but not stated; and the poem concludes with a prayer of two stanzas. The poem's structure resembles the sort of loose, meditative form which we have become used to in such poems as Yeats's 'Among School Children,' but it is a most unusual one for the seventeenth century:

> They are all gone into the world of light!
> > And I alone sit ling'ring here;
> Their very memory is fair and bright,
> > And my sad thoughts doth clear.
>
> It glows and glitters in my cloudy breast
> > Like stars upon some gloomy grove,
> Or those faint beams in which this hill is drest,
> > After the Sun's remove.
>
> I see them walking in an air of glory,
> > Whose light doth trample on my days:
> My days, which are at best but dull and hoary,
> > Meer glimmering and decays.
>
> O holy hope! and high humility
> > High as the Heavens above!
> These are your walks, and you have show'd them me
> > To kindle my cold love.
>
> Dear, beauteous death! the jewel of the just,
> > Shining no where, but in the dark;
> What mysteries do lie beyond thy dust;
> > Could man outlook that mark!
>
> He that hath found some fledged bird's nest, may know
> > At first sight, if the bird be flown;
> But what fair well, or grove he sings in now,
> > That is to him unknown.

And yet, as Angels in some brighter dreams
    Call to the soul, when man doth sleep:
So some strange thoughts transcend our wonted themes,
    And into glory peep.

If a star were cónfined into a tomb
    Her captive flames must needs burn there;
But when the hand that lockt her up, gives room,
    She'll shine through all the sphere.

O Father of eternal life, and all
    Created glories under thee!
Resume thy spirit from this world of thrall
    Into true liberty.

Either disperse these mists, which blot and fill
    My pérspective (still) as they pass
Or else remove me hence unto that hill,
    Where I shall need no glass.

I should like to call attention to two other things about that remarkable poem. I do not know of an earlier passage in English poetry in which the reader is asked to respond to the details of a specific, privately-observed natural landscape in such a way as in the lines, 'Or those faint beams in which this hill is drest, / After the Sun's remove'—as if the afterglow on *this* hill were different from that on any other, and the reader must imagine and respond to an individual, natural peculiarity which only the speaker has seen. And I know of few poetic prayers that seem more authentic or that have less to do with a death wish than the firm final either/or of this poem. What the speaker prays for (and almost demands) is true liberty and the continuation of his vital vision: the method and the place of it no longer matter very much.

A number of years before his death T. S. Eliot is

reported[21] to have said he thought of writing a book to be entitled 'The Fruitfulness of Misunderstanding.' The central idea was that many of the significant changes in poetry have occurred when a writer who is attempting to imitate another or others, through misunderstanding of his model or models creates inadvertently something new. The specific cases Eliot intended to develop, as I remember it, were Coleridge's misunderstanding of German philosophers, Poe's misunderstanding of Coleridge, Baudelaire's and the French *symbolistes'* misunderstanding of Poe, and Eliot's own misunderstanding of the French writers. It is worth remarking that in each of Eliot's examples a writer of some genius, outside or on the periphery of a culture—a foreigner or a provincial—is responsible for the fruitful misunderstanding and the new creation. Eliot's concept seems to apply fairly accurately to the cases of Crashaw and Vaughan. I am willing to believe Mario Praz's assurances[22] that in his imitations of Marino and other Italian poets, Crashaw created something different from and in some respects better than his models; and I feel sure that what Vaughan did with Herbert's poetry follows Eliot's pattern. Both of the seventeenth-century poets were relatively ignored in their own times. Crashaw was admired by Cowley and later barely tolerated by Pope, but except for such secret admirers as Thomas Traherne, Vaughan's published volumes seem to have sunk virtually without a trace. Yet in their fruitful misunderstandings and their new creations, both poets anticipated significantly developments far beyond seventeenth-century England. In the nineteenth and twentieth centuries they became creative parts of the living tradition of English poetry.

CHAPTER V

The Alchemical Ventriloquist:
Andrew Marvell

IF no other English poet of any significance ever took
so much from another as Henry Vaughan did from
George Herbert, I think it likely that no other good
seventeenth-century poet took so much from so many
English poets as did Andrew Marvell. Unlike Vaughan,
almost his exact contemporary, Marvell, the son of a
moderately Puritan conforming minister whom Fuller
described as 'Most *facetious* in his *discourse*, yet *grave* in his
carriage,' was in no sense a provincial. Both from his
writings and from what we know of his life he seems, only
a bit paradoxically, to have been both centrally English
and one of the most cosmopolitan poets of his time. After
seven or eight years at Trinity College, Cambridge, he
spent most of the civil war years travelling on the con-
tinent, in Holland, France, Italy, and Spain. As tutor to
Cromwell's ward and to the Lord General Fairfax's
daughter, and later as Latin Secretary during Cromwell's
last years, Marvell was near enough to the centres of
power to observe them clearly. When he was M.P. for
Hull (from 1659 until his death in 1678) and when he
went on diplomatic missions to Holland, Russia, Denmark, and Sweden, Marvell saw clearly enough the gap
between ceremonial appearances and corrupt or comic
realities, both personal and private, in the Court and
Parliaments of Charles II.

Of all the many candidates for heirs of both Donne and

130

Jonson, Marvell's claims may well be the best. One of his earliest datable poems, 'Flecknoe, An English Priest at Rome,' shows that he had read and could imitate Donne's Satires; he was still quoting from Donne in his late prose satires. Except in the verse satires, however, he never approaches Donne's harshness of sound; in fact, a number of his lyrics are among the most elegant of the Jonsonian variety. In 'Tom May's Death' Marvell introduced the authoritative ghost of Jonson as the judge of Tom May's 'servile wit, and mercenary pen' and the expeller of May from the Elysian fields, and Marvell's 'Upon Appleton House' is the most ambitious and the most impressive of the descendants of Jonson's 'To Penshurst.' But if Marvell is heir of Donne and Jonson, he is also, as J. B. Leishman's *The Art of Marvell's Poetry*[1] demonstrates, the heir of almost everybody else, too. Although one may not find convincing every one of the possible sources of Marvell's verse which Leishman cited, the general pattern like the mass of the evidence, is almost overwhelming. Of the poets with which I have been most concerned in this volume, for example, Marvell mastered so well the gentlemanly tone and wit represented (and partly established) by Suckling that in *The Rehearsal Transpros'd*, as the first writer to defend the 'Good Old Cause' in the tones of a witty, playgoing Restoration gentleman, Marvell got 'all the laughers' and even Charles II momentarily on his side. He used a similar tone (and a crucial image from Suckling's *Aglaura*) in his poem 'Daphnis and Chloe.' For Lovelace's *Lucasta* Marvell wrote an odd and witty prefatory poem that pays more attention to Lovelace's masculine critics and feminine admirers than to his poetry, and he also took a central image from Lovelace for 'The Unfortunate Lover.'

Marvell's 'To his Coy Mistress' is the only competitor of Herrick's 'Corrina's going a-Maying' for the title of the richest English *carpe diem* poem. Carew, whose literary polish sometimes anticipates Marvell, he seems to have known as the author of 'To G. N. from Wrest' as well as the lyrics. *The Temple* was published in the same year that Marvell went up to Herbert's college, and I think Marvell's 'The Coronet,' an impressive religious poem concerning the difficulties in writing religious poetry, owes a good deal to Herbert's 'A Wreath.' Marvell probably knew Crashaw personally, since Crashaw was resident at Cambridge during all the seven or eight years Marvell was there; he used Crashaw's poetry, too—most obviously in 'Eyes and Tears,' where he gave a Latin version of his stanza on St. Mary Magdalen. There is no evidence that Marvell knew Vaughan or Vaughan's poetry, but as Leishman remarked, 'On a Drop of Dew' is nearer to Vaughan's 'The Waterfall' than to any other poem of the century;[2] and Marvell rivaled Vaughan in natural description.

But there were also so many others. (Marvell's practice draws attention to how extremely selective my considera-tion of the 'heirs' of Donne and Jonson has been.) In his poem on the death of Lord Hastings published in *Lachrymae Musarum* (1649), a volume that also contained tributes by Herrick and Denham, Marvell showed that he was alert to the possibilities of the 'new' poetry of Denham and Waller at the same moment when Dryden was still trying to shock with the most tasteless of 'strong lines.' Marvell continued to make use of Waller's poetry, in his later satires as well as his lyrics, and he took sig-nificant contributions from Davenant, Cowley, and es-pecially Cleveland. He seems to have taken things, too, from such relative amateurs as Mildmay Fane and Lord Fairfax as well as from such great figures of the past as Sidney, Spenser, and Shakespeare. And he quoted from Milton's poetry for thirty years, in one of his earliest as well as one of his latest datable poems. Moreover, Marvell's debt to French poetry is one of the largest of his time: to Théophile de Viau and Saint-Amant for more than themes and *libertin* poses and the uses of eight-syllable lines, and perhaps too to Tristan L'Hermite and Georges de Scudéry—and he translated into Latin four of Georges de Brébeuf's lines. And this is the same poet whom T. S. Eliot called the 'most Latin' of all the seventeenth-century poets, who wrote earlier Latin versions of two of his best English poems as well as the best Horatian Ode in English. Modern readers may find all this dazzling, if not discouraging. But no one should conclude that Marvell was simply a poet who had shored a great many fragments against his ruin. If Marvell was something of a ventriloquist who momentarily caught any number of voices, he was also even more of an alchemist who mysteriously transmuted almost everything he touched to a gold stamped with his individual hallmark. As with some other notable poetic magpies, the remarkable thing is not how much he borrowed or stole, but how confidently he brought 'the booty home' and made it his own.

That ability is related to the fact that Marvell's interest in the proprieties and possibilities of literary forms and genres seems as intense as some later poets' interest in their own personalities. Something of the scope of Marvell's art can be glimpsed in the range of his rhetorical and poetic forms: meditations, complaints, persuasions, 'praises' or encomiums, satires or libels, descriptions of figures or landscapes, a definition, an epitaph, an heroic ode, dialogues or debates, a framed monologue, songs with or without frames, and 'Upon Appleton House,' that extraordinary poem in which, under the disguise of a traditional 'country house poem' that compliments a man or family by means of a description of the owner's house (articulated within the general framework of a guided tour of the house and grounds), Marvell managed to include all his major themes as well as a dazzling display of his rhetorical inventions and transformations—even to touches of the masque and the heroic.[3]

Readers who find the continued contemplation of such matters distracting may wish to consider the poems in terms of a smaller, more comfortable number of categories. If they are historically minded and remember Hobbes, they may see that most of Marvell's poetry falls within a sort of pastoral grouping (extended to include the Mower poems and the garden and country-house poems), more than most readers recognize within the satiric or 'scommatic,' and that kind of heroic is used consistently in the Cromwell poems and intermittently in the Fairfax poems. Probably a larger number of readers will find it more natural to consider the poems in terms of their general subjects. It is surprising to discover how many can be described as predominantly concerned with love or religion or politics. (In Marvell's verse the ethical is usually associated with one of those three.) Some of the poems are notable for the odd relations they assume or suggest between love and religion, religion and politics, or even politics and love. The most popular of Marvell's poems today either clearly fit into one of these categories or mark the transition from one to another: 'To his Coy Mistress,' 'The Definition of Love,' 'The Garden,' 'The Coronet.' 'On a Drop of Dew,' 'Bermudas,' 'An Horatian Ode

upon Cromwell's Return from Ireland,' perhaps even 'The Picture of Little T. C. in a Prospect of Flowers.'

With a poet so conscious of literary precedents and traditions and individual styles as Marvell, we may find that almost every poem suggests new possibilities—and perhaps a new bibliography. But it is dangerous to assume that this gentleman whose poetic elegance sometimes seems nearly absolute is following any *one* tradition or interpretation. We must pay the closest attention to the details of Marvell's art (to his uses of poetic structures as well as diction, his momentary evocations, his qualifications) if we are to read well his best poems. Otherwise we may find that we have followed themes or ideas or images into any number of learned or curious by-ways but that we have somehow missed the poems themselves. In the hope that a fairly close look at one poem and some of the problems in its interpretation may prove suggestive for the reading of other poems, I shall consider 'The Garden,' one of Marvell's finest poems and one which has been considerably and ingeniously over-read in our time.

In so far as we know, Charles Lamb, Emerson, and Poe were among the earliest enthusiastic readers of Marvell's poems,[4] and that bit of knowledge seems significant. Discovered by the Romantics, admitted to the pantheon of Romantic and Victorian poetry (and compared to Shelley) by Palgrave in 1861, 'The Garden' is still usually read as a Romantic poem. The usual procedure seems to be roughly as follows: The reader responds intensely to those three stanzas, v through vii, which describe ecstatic fulfilment. Having responded, he then leaps intuitively to the certainty that those stanzas *are* the poem, and that they are 'profound' and serious in every way.

(After all, the sensitive and intelligent reader responded to them, didn't he?) The reader assumes that no 'true poet' could possibly create such sensuous and evocative stanzas except as the expression of his highest ideals, or primary imagination, or, perhaps, 'true self.' (Of the English Romantics, I believe only Byron would have seriously doubted such a formulation—but Byron is not particularly influential these days.) Certain of his central response or 'truth,' the reader usually either ignores the rest of the poem or else attempts to work it out on the assumption that the whole should be as serious and profound as he thinks stanzas v through vii are.

Certain other modern tendencies should probably be distinguished from the Romantic. Most important is the assumption that complexity is always preferable to simplicity in good poetry—or even, the more complex the better. Related to that assumption but distinguishable from it is the notion that a poem may justly be valued in direct proportion to the quantity of intellectual and literary history which it can be demonstrated to contain. Even stranger are the notions that tradition is always a good thing; that a 'traditional' reading is always to be accepted in preference to an 'untraditional'; and that, where more than one tradition must be recognized, the older or more orthodox tradition must be the predominant one in a good poem. Since nearly everyone agrees that 'The Garden' is a good poem, a number of readers, often sensitive and intelligent ones, have expended an enormous amount of ingenuity in attempts to demonstrate its enormous complexity in language and attitude and both its complexity and orthodoxy in philosophical and theological doctrine.

Dryden, who may have been taking a smack at George

Herbert when he wrote about poets who 'torture one poor word ten thousand ways,' could hardly, I believe, have anticipated William Empson's reading of Marvell's 'Garden.' But Empson's subtleties are more than equalled by the readers who have found key 'sources' of, or analogues to, the poem's central 'meaning' or 'doctrine' in an extraordinarily impressive range of figures and writings: Buddha and The Canticles and the Mass, Plato and Plotinus and 'Hermes Trismegistus,' St. Paul and the Kabbala, St. Bonaventura and St. Thomas Aquinas, Hugh of St. Victor and the *Ancrene Riwle*, Ficino and Leone Ebreo, Henry More and John Smith, Spinoza, Blake and Keats, Alfred North Whitehead and John Dewey. No one would deny that most of these contain profundities or that many provide either images of or patterns for the good life—or dreams of perfection. One could even suggest that plausible analogies can be discovered (or constructed) between the profound writings associated with these names and stanzas v through vii of 'The Garden'— if we take those stanzas in isolation. If one admits all this and still persists in the conviction that the learned analogies have usually proved misleading about the poem as a whole, one should at least try to determine how the readers have gone wrong.

I think the first mistake (to repeat) is to interpret the poem by means of the three magic stanzas instead of reading those stanzas within the context of the poem. Close to it, both in error and frequency, is the tendency for a reader to develop an elaborate interpretation of the poem with little or no consideration of the probabilities that the same man could have written the reader's poem and Marvell's other poetry and prose. Of course it is theoretically possible for a poet to write a poem utterly unlike his other work, *sui generis* in ideas and values and language; but to assume lightly that any one poem is such a work seems to me extremely dangerous. In general, I think it a good idea to have read most of a writer's work before one starts writing about individual poems, and to keep as much of that work in mind as one possibly can in readiness for those occasions in which one passage may provide a helpful gloss upon another. I believe, for example, that anyone who has read carefully Marvell's prose as well as his other poems would be unlikely to interpret 'The Garden' as the systematic mystical meditation of a Roman Catholic religious.

A third error may be the oddest and most debilitating of all. In a critical age when the word 'tone' has been used incessantly and when 'wit' has become a term of almost unmitigated praise, few readers have bothered to evaluate —or even to notice—the wit of 'The Garden.' The possibility that the sounds and rhythms of the poem might help one to determine the degrees of seriousness of specific passages has very often been ignored. The lines of 'The Garden' have frequently been read as if they were spoken by a preacher or formal philosopher or a nineteenth-century poet instead of by an oddly individual speaker within a seventeenth-century poem.

Frank Kermode's essay, 'The Argument of Marvell's "Garden",'[5] and the final chapter of J. B. Leishman's *The Art of Marvell's Poetry* (1966) are exceptions to most of what I have said: both Kermode and Leishman considered the poem as a whole, both knew Marvell's other works, and both got most of the jokes. (Only my differences with some of their conclusions make me think I still have something to say.) Anyone who has read their essays —or even merely read much in Renaissance literature—

must realize that the seventeenth-century literary woods
were full of gardens. There was Eden, of course, and the
mystical gardens of the Canticles and of the Virgin. More
important than the Virgin's for most English Protestants
were the secular gardens of 'retired life,' some of Horatian
or more or less neo-stoic design; and those gardens could
easily blend into very real gardens (such as that of Lord
Fairfax at Nun Appleton, Yorkshire), which could, in
turn, represent the temporary or permanent places of
retirement and pleasure for an active and distinguished
man—or for, say, his daughter's tutor, who had not
chosen to fight in the English Civil War. And there were
other gardens—'*libertin*,' 'naturalist,' 'Epicurean,' or
what-have-you-which were symbols for sensuous and even
sensual fulfilment, often with a lady present and willing
and 'unnatural' concepts such as honour banished. Each
of these gardens could be considered, seriously or playfully, a 'paradise,' lost or found, but on differing occasions
and by different men. It is hardly safe to assume that
Marvell was ignorant or unconscious of any of these (it
seems to have been his delight to write on subjects and in
genres which possessed multiple and often contradictory
literary traditions); it is even less safe to assume that *his*
'garden' is adequately represented by any one of the
traditional types: for Marvell's 'Garden' is a poem rather
than a place or a 'type,' and what the poem is and does is
what we wish to discover.

With 'The Garden,' as with most other seventeenth-
century poems, it is helpful to pay some attention to the
poem's shape and the way the 'argument' is organized.
If we look at the shape of Marvell's English poem, we
notice that those famous stanzas v-vii that celebrate the
ecstasies which define 'What wond'rous life in this I

lead'—stanzas that are certainly central to the poem if not equivalent to it—are framed by stanzas which are witty distortions, first, of classical myth, and then, of the biblical account of Eden. With such obvious symmetry, one might expect more. But the poem begins with three introductory stanzas which claim that the garden contains a truer fame, quiet, innocence, and amorousness than the world outside; and it ends with only one: that concerning the gardener, the floral sundial, and the industrious bee. With a poet who cared so much about formal elements as Marvell did, one might ask, why? And for our reading of the poem it is more important to ask, how does the formal imbalance work? If the poem succeeds formally, one might expect that stanza ix alone truly concludes it in a manner somehow related to the way that stanzas i through iii begin it. (The formal problem may be considered an exaggerated analogy to the usual problem of the Italian sonnet: how do those last six lines 'answer' or complete or transform, 'balance' or over-balance—at any rate, *conclude*—those first eight?)

Hortus, Marvell's Latin poem which seems to be an earlier version of the English one, is organized in a different fashion but it substantiates the impression that the beginning and the ending of 'The Garden' were conceived in relationship to each other.[6] Moreover, both poems begin with the rejection of the worlds of ambitious action, urban life, and passionate love, and celebrate a supposed entrance into an entirely new life within the garden. (In *Hortus* the speaker calls himself a 'new citizen' and prays that the 'Leafy citizens' may accept him 'in the flowery kingdom.')[7] Both poems end with almost identical lines concerning time and certain precious hours. Any satisfactory reading of 'The Garden' should attempt to account for the relationship between the beginning and the end.

While I believe, of course, that my hints concerning formal problems are of major importance for the poem, I cannot expect to convince sceptics unless I can demonstrate their relevance in a reading of the poem which more or less convincingly accounts for the way it works and moves. It is not enough with seventeenth-century poems, I think, to develop erudite and plausible 'historical meanings' or to elaborate diagrams and 'spatial forms' unless we can show how the reader is supposed to acquire his knowledge or experience of those constructions as he reads the poems, line by line and stanza by stanza. For the seventeenth-century poems we care most about really do move—not at all like 'Chinese jars in their stillness,' but openly in rhetorical shifts, changing assumptions, resolutions lost or modified. Their 'meanings' cannot be defined by any abstract statement partly because they often concern precisely the process of change from one position to another.

Let us turn to the poem:

> How vainly men themselves amaze
> To win the palm, the oak, or bays;
> And their uncessant labours see
> Crowned from some single herb or tree:
> Whose short and narrow vergèd shade
> Does prudently their toils upbraid;
> While all flowers and all trees do close
> To weave the garlands of repose.

Although I have met few bright students, knowing in the intricacies of modern criticism, who have even smiled at those lines, I find their self-conscious false naïveté very funny. The speaker looks at the incredible labours which men undergo for 'the palm, the oak, or bays' and pretends he thinks that all they want are those 'crowns,' each made from the leaves of only one tree, as shades from the sun—the physical symbols for a doubtful utilitarian purpose rather than the recognition of victory and triumph that the symbols signify. (It is as if one thought the only possible reason anyone could wish to win the Davis cup would be to drink out of it.) But the symbols themselves, short-lived and not really offering much protection from the sun, offer prudent reproof to such toils. And if one merely *rests* in the most pleasant place—a garden—*all* flowers and *all* trees 'close' to weave much handsomer, richer, and more efficient garlands. For readers who live in a society with different status symbols and who are not continually reminded of Renaissance notions concerning mortal and immortal fame, the extravagance and the joke may be less obvious than for a seventeenth-century reader, but we can still recognize both.

In one of his earliest poems, Marvell had had fun with the famous lines on Fame in *Lycidas*: he had expressed the 'frail ambition,' 'The last distemper of the sober brain,' that there had been a witness to assure future ages how he endured his 'martyrdom' when Fleckno recited his hideous verses. But there Marvell presented himself as the gallant man of common sense who had read Donne's Satires and was busy exposing another monstrous aberration. Milton's original lines are more to the point here: Why shouldn't a shepherd 'sport with Amaryllis in the shade' in stead of 'with uncessant care' (Marvell may have remembered Milton's use of 'uncessant') tending the 'shepherd's trade' and strictly meditating 'the thankless Muse?' The answer is clear:

> Fame is the spur that the clear spirit doth raise
> (That last infirmity of noble mind)
> To scorn delights, and live laborious days. . . .
>
> (ll. 70-72)

Even though death may intervene before the great work is completed, Phoebus assures the poet that true fame will be granted by 'all-judging Jove'—in just proportion, manifestly, to the tended trade and meditated Muse. Although the desire for fame may be an 'infirmity,' what it is the spur to is the 'clear spirit' which creates and acts —and is rewarded. Marvell begins 'The Garden' with an extravagant dismissal of all efforts for fame. Instead of being raised, the spirit is advised to relax and give up any attempt for military, civic, or poetic distinction: the whole duty of man here seems summarized in that climactic word, *repose*. The outrageous suavity and the calculated rationality (notice 'prudently') of the lines invite us to smile and warn us of extravagances to come. The poem is going to claim *everything* for a life of infinite leisure in the garden; but the ways in which it makes its claim reveal the urbanity of the poet who created this fictional voice, his recognition of values beyond those which he pretends to dismiss and those which he pretends exhaust all the pleasant and virtuous possibilities of human life.

The exclamatory apostrophe to Quiet and Innocence of stanza ii has a pseudo-operatic quality of sudden discovery:

> Fair Quiet, have I found thee here,[8]
> And Innocence, thy sister dear!
> Mistaken long, I sought you then
> In busy companies of men.
> Your sacred plants, if here below,
> Only among the plants will grow.

> Society is all but rude,
> To this delicious solitude.

Yet if these lines stood alone, we should probably have to take them simply and seriously. After all the theme is hoary: true quiet and innocence do not exist in great places but in the simple life. Our suspicions have, however, already been aroused by stanza i, and they are sustained. This, too, is extravagant. The simple life was usually, in secular literature at least, considered a life in a landscape with *some* figures, the villa or the village away from the centres of power and ambition or the retreat with the mistress, but not the anchorite's, totally divorced from human contact. (And the anchorites, we might remember, usually took a cell in the desert or a pillar, not a pleasant garden, as a place of retirement.) Reading these lines one may come to wonder whether it is really so remarkable that it should be quiet if no one at all is present to make noise. And it is surprising to discover that one may be relatively 'innocent' if one sees no other human beings at all, either to be corrupted by or to harm? The virtue of this 'innocence' is so fugitive that it would find a cloister crowded.

The latent incongruities explode with the final couplet of the stanza:

> Society is all but rude,
> To this delicious solitude.

The marvellously dancing rhythm, the temporal fall of the rhymes with the meanings of 'rude' and 'solitude,' the delicate mock-precision of 'all but,' and the lovely misuse of 'delicious' (perhaps a reminiscence of Crashaw) are the very embodiment of the wit. If one thinks at all about the relationships between 'rude' and 'polished,' between 'society' and life outside of society, one can paraphrase what the lines actually say in a number of ways which, unwittily, make the absurdity obvious: society is almost rustic in comparison to rusticity; the state which polishes is almost rough in comparison to the state of roughness; civilization is almost barbaric in comparison to no civilization. That we may think, in certain times and places and moods, that each paraphrase contains more than a bit of truth in addition to its absurdity is all to the point. Marvell's own phrasing assures us that the speaker must have received the highest possible polish from society before he could formulate the couplet; and he (or the author) knows it. Never has civilization been rejected in a more elegantly civilized fashion. The wit reminds us strongly of values which are beyond the gift of Quiet and Innocence and which were never learned in a garden.

In the third stanza the speaker rejects the beauty of human female figures for the superior 'amorousness' of the trees:

> No white nor red was ever seen
> So am'rous as this lovely green.

The second stanza, with its 'delicious solitude,' has given us fair warning that this is to be no ordinary 'naturalistic' garden of sensuous delight as the lover and his mistress return to nature. But we can hardly have anticipated, I believe, such a bold claim for the total fulfilment of man's amorous nature without the ladies. The speaker 'proves' that the trees are capable of inspiring his passion by his comment on the ordinary lovers who carve their mistresses' names in the bark of the trees:

> Fond lovers, cruel as their flame,
> Cut in these trees their mistress' name.
> Little, alas, they know, or heed,
> How far these beauties hers exceed!

145

> Fair Trees! wheres'e'er your barks I wound,
> No name shall but your own be found.

It takes a very solemn reader indeed no to smile at the figure of the man so in love with the trees that, to express that love, he carves 'Plane,' 'Cypress,' 'Poplar,' and 'Elm' on the corresponding love-objects. (*Hortus* spells it out: precisely those names will be substituted for Naera, Chloe, Faustina, and Corynna.) One horridly surrealist analogy would be a mad lover who carved his mistress's name on his mistress. Almost equally mad is the sentimental botanist with many loves, satisfied in the homage of the carved labels, since no other words could equal the grandeur or the erotic passion of the names themselves.

Stanza iv, continuing the eroticism, turns to the gods and goddesses:

> When we have run our passion's heat,
> Love hither makes his best retreat.
> The gods, that mortal beauty chase,
> Still in a tree did end their race:
> Apollo hunted Daphne so,
> Only that she might laurel grow;
> And Pan did after Syrinx speed,
> Not as a nymph, but for a reed.

Of course Marvell knew the moralizations of the myths. Of course he knew that, although the speaker had supposedly rejected the 'laurel' in the 'bays' of stanza i as something actively to be striven for, *we* in large part value Apollo for the laurel and Pan for the reed. And the idea that the garden is the 'best retreat' of Love after the 'heat' and the 'race' of passion is neat and plausible. (The puns on 'heat' and 'race,' like all of Marvell's best ones, seem inevitable and without strain.) But the extravagance of the word 'Still' assures us that we have not abandoned the realm of conscious and playful exaggeration: 'The gods, that mortal beauty chase, / *Still* in a tree did end their race.' Many of the gods did—and *Hortus* adds Jupiter and Mars to Apollo and Pan—but not all the gods, and not all of the 'races.' And the same sort of exaggeration is present in that word 'Only': 'Apollo hunted Daphne so, / *Only* that she might laurel grow.' It is one thing to claim, as *Hortus* does at one point, that the gods rejoice when the tyrant Love loses his heat and that, although experienced in all the nymphs and goddesses, 'Each one achieves his desires better now in a tree.'[9] It is quite another (and a complete reversal of the myth) to say that all that Apollo ever wanted from Daphne was that she turn to laurel. And that goat-footed Pan sought Syrinx 'Not as a nymph, but for a reed' is even more delightfully absurd. As he has done consistently thus far in the poem, Marvell gets some of his wittiest effects from blandly pretending either to identify a symbol with the thing symbolized or one element of a myth or situation with the clusters of meanings which are truly involved.

It is in stanzas v through vii that the speaker describes in detail the absolute fulfilment within the garden which up until then he has merely claimed to exist:

> What wond'rous life in this I lead!
> Ripe apples drop about my head;
> The luscious clusters of the vine
> Upon my mouth do crush their wine;
> The nectarine, and curious peach,
> Into my hands themselves do reach;
> Stumbling on melons, as I pass,
> Ensnared with flowers, I fall on grass.
>
> Meanwhile the mind, from pleasure less,
> Withdraws into its happiness:

147

The mind, that ocean where each kind
Does straight its own resemblance find;
Yet it creates, transcending these,
Far other worlds, and other seas;
Annihilating all that's made
To a green thought in a green shade.

Here at the fountain's sliding foot,
Or at some fruit-tree's mossy root,
Casting the body's vest aside,
My soul into the boughs does glide:
There like a bird it sits, and sings,
Then whets, and combs its silver wings;
And, till prepared for longer flight,
Waves in its plumes the various light.

We should certainly be grateful here for all the useful
learning and special knowledge that we can get. But we
must make sure that the learning is truly relevant and that
it will help us to read these stanzas instead of distracting
us from them. It may be interesting to know that the
Greek root of *melon* means 'apple' and that the roots of the
words for other English fruits here may also mean 'apple'
in other languages; but if we get too many apples in
stanza v we may miss the more important point that for
this ecstasy the pleasantly aggressive fruits[10] systemati-
cally overwhelm differing parts of the man's body (head,
mouth, hands, legs, and feet) without any willful or even
masculine behaviour on his part. And although 'Stum-
bling,' 'Ensnared' and 'fall' may make us think of sin and
Adam's fall in another Garden, we should recognize that
the chief points of the stanza are that this is *not* Eden[11]
and this is not sinful: *this* 'fall' is pleasant and innocent,
on grass rather than into sin, a truly 'wond'rous' ecstatic
fulfilment of the body without overt sexuality. That is

why the speaker prefers the trees to the mistresses and the gods now prefer their trees or reeds to their former loves.

Similarly, I think we would do well to forget the 'ambiguities' which have been found in 'Meanwhile the mind, from pleasure less, / Withdraws into its happiness.' It seems obvious that the ecstasies are in an ascending order (reversing the descent from the crowns and garlands to the loves of the opening stanzas), and that the most important thing the lines mean is that the mind withdraws from the lesser pleasure of the body to experience its own separate and greater pleasure in its ecstasy of knowledge and creative thought. If the structure of the poem counts for anything, the lines cannot possibly mean that the mind is 'reduced' or 'lessened' by pleasure, for the entire movement is towards the extravagant claim that each aspect of man enjoys its highest pleasure in the garden.

The single most important thing of all to notice about the three stanzas is, I believe, that they neatly divide man's being, not into the difficult but conventional body and soul, but into a more divisive body, mind, and soul. Their mischievously witty claim is that the completely separable perfect pleasures of body, mind, and soul can be experienced here on earth, simultaneously and without strain[12]—and, according to the poem through stanza vi, supposedly without end. Had Marvell wished chiefly for credibility, had he intended his readers seriously to consider these stanzas the expression of the highest possible 'Garden-state,' embodying a paradisiacal perfection outside of time and human measure, he would, I think, have handled that claim quite differently. If, like Milton in his description of Eden, he had wished to emphasize that all the aspects of man were truly fulfilled in paradise, he would have shown the union, not the separation, of body, mind, and soul; or he might, like innumerable other writers in their serious or playful descriptions of 'perfection' and ecstatic fulfilment, have emphasized one sort —sensuous, mental, or spiritual—as truly 'transcending,' surpassing and including, the other forms. In those cases, however, we have other poems: serious descriptions of unfallen man or serious or playful descriptions of the 'perfections' to be sought in the libertine paradise or in the mental paradises of knowledge and creativity or in the spiritual paradises of song and mystical illumination. But 'The Garden' is claiming *all*. By that very extravagance and by the strict compartmentalization of the three ecstasies, Marvell dramatizes precisely the strains which the poem's surface claims do not exist, and he places the heaviest possible burden on the speaker's simple acquiescence: *while* the body, 'Ensnared with flowers,' has fallen on the grass, the mind is 'Annihilating all that's made / To a green thought in a green shade': and at the same or similar moment, 'Casting the body's vest aside,' the soul glides into the boughs:

> There like a bird it sits, and sings,
> Then whets, and combs its silver wings;
> And, till prepared for longer flight,
> Waves in its plumes the various light.[13]

It is within stanza vii that time first enters significantly into the life of the garden; until then, apart from the witty emphasis on the simultaneity of the ecstasies, time has been merely part of that world of action, ambition, society, and passion from which 'we' have retreated, we had thought, forever. But here, as it 'sits, and sings' and 'Waves in its plumes the various light' of this world, the soul knowingly awaits the time when it is prepared for the 'longer flight' into the unvarying light of eternity. That very modification of the absoluteness of the former claims —the recognition that there is a flight longer than any the soul can know in the garden—gives a reality and poignance to the stanza beyond anything we have met so far. It is at this moment that the poem nearly becomes something like the 'serious' poem that many readers assume it to be throughout. The longing for fulfilment, which has been just beneath the surface even if we 'know' that all the divisions of man's nature cannot experience complete and eternal ecstasy on earth, must be recognized openly here. But this note is touched only for a moment.

Stanza viii, with its witty reversal of Genesis ii, 18 ('And the Lord God said, it is not good that the man should be alone; I will make him an help meet for him') returns us to the world of laughter, paradox, mortality, and measure:

> Such was that happy Garden-state,
> While man there walked without a mate:
> After a place so pure, and sweet,
> What other help could yet be meet!
> But 'twas beyond a mortal's share
> To wander solitary there:
> Two paradises 'twere in one
> To live in Paradise alone.

St. Ambrose and St. Jerome may have literally believed that man would have been happier without a mate, but, despite all the misogynist literature of the ancient and medieval and Renaissance worlds, such a belief was never central nor widely held by poets. This particular poem, moreover, was written neither by nor for a St. Jerome. More to the point are the play on 'mate' and 'meet' and the self-consciously blasphemous reversal of the biblical accounts both of the creation of woman and the loss of Eden. The implications are inescapable: that the chief cause for the loss of Paradise was the creation of woman rather than sin; and that, simply by returning to a garden, solitary man can recover the state of innocence. These extravagances, along with the dancing movement of the couplets in which they are conveyed, assure us that, whatever the speaker's sexual condition or private beliefs, he is not seriously proposing for our approbation the notion of Adam as the happy hermaphrodite. The gaiety and the reminder of the biblical account of Paradise provide a comic perspective on some assumptions that may underlie the seductive ecstasies that have gone before: the notions that heterosexual relations are 'unnatural' and that no more than one man should ever have existed. Whatever the opinions of individual theologians and philosophers, most readers of poetry eventually see limitations in notions of 'perfection' based on such assumptions.

Stanza viii goes so far that it almost undercuts all the claims which have been made for the garden. It may seem for a moment that the perception of any values whatsoever for the solitary and contemplative life within the place of ordered natural beauty is a delusion, that the 'real' life of man can only be found in the worlds of public action, social colloquy, and the pursuit of love. But the concluding stanza modifies that extravagance, too. It is, once again, with the introduction of time that we touch a wider reality:

> How well the skillful gard'ner drew
> Of flowers and herbs this dial new;
> Where from above the milder sun
> Does through a fragrant zodiac run;

And, as it works, th' industrious bee
Computes its time as well as we.
How could such sweet and wholesome hours
Be reckoned but with herbs and flowers!

Since the first stanza began with 'How vainly,' it is
proper that the final stanza should begin with 'How well.'
But what is done so well is not the retreat from all action
to solitary contemplation but the 'skilful' construction by
the gardener of a dial which measures time. Here, for the
first time since those pursuing gods in stanza iv do we
see a figure in human shape that moves purposefully; for
the first time since stanza i do we hear of anything that
labours or works: the gardener has 'drawn' the dial; the
sun 'runs' through a 'fragrant zodiac': the 'industrious
bee' 'Computes its time' 'as it works.' And we, too, are
invited to the mild labour of 'computing' or 'reckoning'
'sweet and wholesome hours' with an objectivity and a
sense of multiple possibilities which we could not possibly
have summoned at the moments of ecstatic fulfilment that
seemed eternal. The dial implies not only time, but the
vicissitudes of times; it measures for us only our pleasant
hours of retreat within the garden when the sun runs
through the 'fragrant zodiac,' neither those of cloud or
night within the solitary life nor those of the less 'mild'
sun of the world of action beyond the garden. And the
herbs and flowers are proper for reckoning our sunny
hours within the garden not only because they are 'sweet
and wholesome,' but also because the grass withers and
the flowers fade. (The phrase *brevibus plantis* of *Hortus*,
1. 50, encourages me to believe that I am not reading into
the poem meanings which Marvell did not intend to be
there.) The final stanza truly balances and 'answers' those
three introductory stanzas as well as concludes the entire

poem in its summary of our experiences within the garden: they have been in time, not in eternity; and however pleasant, they are only an evanescent part of the life that we value, and a smaller part still of the life that we live.

I hope that no one will think I have created a 'Marvell's "Garden" for tired business men'—although perhaps Lord Fairfax was, according to elevated seventeenth-century standards, something of a 'tired businessman.' I am more nearly intimidated by the thought of a modest reader who considers my reading overly elaborate and may wish to remark, 'I just thought Marvell was a man who liked gardens.' But whatever the criticisms, and however inferior in profound philosophical and religious meanings my reading may be, I am convinced that it comes close to the poem that Marvell actually wrote. I believe that in 'The Garden' Marvell was trying to do something other than to express or dramatize eternal philosophical or religious choices, and I also believe that he was doing more than expressing personal taste in horticulture. Of course the poem recognizes the absurdities and the losses associated with the mindless pursuit of the active life: no literate poet in the mid-seventeenth century could have been unaware of them. But more immediately important for the poem, I think, were the extravagant claims for the retired life which were made, with more or less seriousness, by devotees of pastoral poetry, neo-stoic gentlemen, mystical contemplatives, and libertines alike, in an age which had experienced and remembered the dangers and horrors of civil war: the claims that one mode of the retired life exhausted all the 'real,' the valuable possibilities of human life. By pretending to accept precisely such claims and by pushing them to their ultimately absurd limits, Marvell wrote a poem which is both one of the wittiest of the age and which contains one of the age's most moving accounts of the dream of absolute fulfilment. But the end of the poem is inevitable: the gentle and eminently civilized recognition that retirement to a garden may provide truly sweet and wholesome hours—and a marvellous occasion for a poem —but not a way of life.

CHAPTER VI

Private Taste and Public Judgement:
Andrew Marvell

i

THE larger number of Marvell's modern admirers,
I believe, have come to the poems with the assumption that the relatively short, supposedly 'private'
poem, uncommitted to cause or action, is the most
desirable or highest kind of poetry, and they seem to
assume that Marvell must have agreed with them. But a
number of Marvell's poems, when we consider them
closely, may shock us with their kind of 'privacy.' However modern Marvell may seem in his apparently self-
conscious and experimental aestheticism, he is very much
a representative of the Renaissance amateur gentleman in
writing so many of his poems, in so far as we can tell, with
no thought whatsoever of having them printed. Most of
them seem not even to have circulated in manuscript, and
the posthumous publication of the bulk of the poetry in
1681 was occasioned only by a complicated legal and
financial manœuvre on the part of some business ac-
quaintances who neither recognized nor cared about the
poem's literary qualities.[1] I may be forgetting obvious
instances, but I cannot think of a poet after Marvell who
wrote poetry in English of the first rank without at least
considering its publication or distribution. (One thinks of
Emily Dickinson, but by her early submission of a few
poems, she showed that she could at least imagine her
'private' lyrics being printed.) Although some moderns
can hardly imagine how anyone might write good poetry

without intending publication or, short of personal or public disaster, how anyone might quit writing magnificent 'private' poetry after he had shown that he could do so, there were advantages to Marvell's old-fashioned position. At least he never seems to have anticipated the peculiar difficulties of some modern poets who assume both that valuable poetry should be essentially private and inward in subject and style and also that the poet must be 'dedicated' and 'professional,' since only his identity as poet (a special form of 'the artist') provides a justification for his existence. Sometimes these assumptions almost appear to be a formula for self-destruction. Should the poet fail to keep up, in both quantity and quality, his production of 'private' poems, he may think he has provided public evidence of personal and spiritual failure. As a result, he is subjected to extraordinary tensions and strains, including a pressure to exploit ruthlessly his private experience. Marvell never seems to have imagined that his personal salvation depended upon his continued productions of poetic masterpieces. I do not believe it ever occurred to him to worry about how he could write a *second* 'To his Coy Mistress' or 'The Garden'; the attitudes and anxieties which such a concern imply might well have made it impossible for him to write the first ones.

But if these poems are in one way more 'private' than anything we can easily imagine today, they also use the rhetorical devices of an age supremely conscious of the powers and problems of the social, and particularly the persuasive, uses of language. The mistress may be anonymous if not imaginary, but she is addressed most formally and even syllogistically. The speaking voice pretends to speak only to his mistress, or to Quiet and Innocence and the Fair Trees, or to God, or to meditate or define according to recognizable and circumspect patterns. Even in the most 'private' poems we can never safely assume that the main import of the poem is simply some shadowy urge for 'self-expression,' for almost every one of them assumes an immediate rhetorical object of address as well as the possibility of a larger group of 'overhearers,' however difficult either may be to define precisely. (We shall, incidentally, read 'The Definition of Love' very differently depending on whether we assume its immediate rhetorical audience to be a lady who glories in an ideal and unconsummated love, a lady who has hoped for a more ordinary love, or even the Resolved Soul.[2]) And nearly all of the most 'private' poems represent or imitate at least a momentary decision or judgement related to the rival claims of the retired and the active lives.

But these poems do seem most 'private' in comparison with the ones in which Marvell celebrates or derides public men and events. Until recently the conventional opinion has been clear about the contrast: Marvell's good poems were the 'private' ones, and the public poems, with the exception of 'An Horatian Ode,' were bad. Marvell could even serve as the prime exemplary proof for the 'cultural break,' the 'dissociation of sensibility' which set in at 1660: before that date, supposedly, Marvell wrote the poems which we all admire; afterwards, he was the victim of politics, satire, and an age (the beginning of our modern one) when thought and 'feeling' (it was rarely clear whether 'feeling' meant sensation or emotion) were hopelessly split apart. I think it remarkable that an age which saw some of the finest work of Milton, Dryden, Rochester, Traherne, Congreve, Swift, Pope, and Gay could for long have been lamented as marking the onset of poetic or literary darkness. One can understand that readers who admire most the relatively short, supposedly 'private,' tightly organized poem which uses low or middle diction and dramatizes emotional choices may view the new age with a sense of loss. But they should be careful that in their defense of private and personal values they do not attribute too much to abstract and hazily apprehended social or historical forces. Actually, few of the most interesting poets of the earlier seventeenth century wrote such poems for long; and the dates when they ceased, like their reasons for ceasing, differed widely. Is the fact that Donne wrote remarkably few poems, secular or religious, during the last twenty years of his life really to be attributed to the unsatisfactory cultural climate between 1611 and 1631? Can anyone seriously maintain that Henry Vaughan's failure of inspiration after the second part of *Silex Scintillans* in 1655 is directly related to the notable social or political or aesthetic changes in Brecknockshire immediately after that date? Like a number of the others, Marvell seems to have been a gentleman who for a time wrote a kind of poetry that we have come to admire greatly. Although he was, with Jonson and Milton, one of the most 'literary' poets of the century, unlike them he conceived of himself neither as a professional nor as a dedicated poet. When the inspiration or the occasion for a particular kind of verse was past, his choice seems to have been either to quit writing verse altogether or to turn to a new kind of poetry.

I do not mean to deny that there were significant changes during the seventeenth century—social, religious, and political, economic, philosophical, and linguistic, as well as literary—to the point that it is possible, by means of selected passages of prose or poetry, to demonstrate what seem to be two different 'worlds,' an Elizabethan one at the beginning and a modern one at the end. I am only objecting to the tendency to exaggerate the changes (it is also possible by means of other selected passages of poetry and prose to demonstrate a number of continuities), to localize them precisely in one year or even decade, and to attribute all the literary changes to large, impersonal 'movements'—as if all talented writers were hapless victims of an age rather than, literarily at least, among the creators of it.

From fairly early in the seventeenth century a number of the poets began to cultivate intensely the Jonsonian part of their inheritance. There were probably manifold reasons. Fashions have a way of changing even faster than manners, and both 'strong lines' and attempts at bluff persuasions and arguments could quickly come to seem tiresomely old-fashioned. Smoothness and polish might easily be preferred to roughness and 'strength.' The very ideal of the passionate and markedly individual (if not eccentric) voice might come to be viewed with suspicion and some distaste. The period heard a large number of such voices, in political and religious controversies as well as in literature, voices immensely concerned with important issues and strongly committed to specific public and private positions. It would certainly be understandable if, both before and after bloodshed and revolutions, many men came to prefer voices which attempted, or at least pretended to, a measured and balanced tone appropriate to rational and compromising public judgements.

As nearly as we can tell, Marvell's practice differed from the normal responses of his age chiefly in agility and elegance. But we really have remarkably little evidence for dating most of Marvell's best poems. Although it is sensible to assume that 'The Garden' and the Mower poems are probably associated with 'Upon Appleton House' and Marvell's residence with Lord Fairfax from 1651 to about 1653, and also to assume that the poems concerning love are those of a relatively young man (dating roughly from the same period or earlier), we have no way of knowing. And Marvell's concern with traditions and genres seems so intense and in some ways so modern that I am haunted by the thought that he might have found himself in a position resembling André Malraux's description of the modern painter's: possessed of an imaginary museum filled with the works of all ages and cultures, and therefore capable both of imitating anything and of concentrating on what he thinks the essence of art (rather than on art within its normal contexts and functions), quite apart from the usual chronologies. Is it possible that Marvell's interior anthology of the Latin, English, and French poems which he had mastered served him as an everpresent reminder of the aesthetic possibilities of past forms and genres, and that he might have written some of his most admired lyrics, perhaps with a good deal of nostalgia, shortly before his death in 1678? It is a mischievous question, calculated to disturb our assumptions of historical certainty, and I am sorry that I do not really think an affirmative answer to it is likely. Still, we might remember that few literary historians or critics thought it likely that anything resembling Thomas Traherne's poetry could have been written during the Restoration before some of Traherne's manuscripts were discovered and his first volume of poetry published in 1903. (We cannot dodge the latter embarrassment simply by assuming that Traherne was a provincial recluse, unaware of his times. He may have begun humbly enough in Hereford, but he took three degrees at Oxford, he had read his Hobbes as well as the Cambridge- and neo-Platonists, and he was chaplain to Sir Orlando Bridgeman, the Lord Keeper.) And what about Edward Taylor?

Certainly, the poems of Marvell that we can date do not support the thesis that the fine lyric poet was suddenly changed into a writer of political poems and satires. One of the earliest of Marvell's datable poems was the rather brutal, if funny, satire on 'Flecke.' 'An Horatian Ode,' Marvell's finest poem on public affairs, was written in the early summer of 1650, before the poems associated with Appleton House. Both the lovely 'Bermudas' and the comic political libel 'The Character of Holland' seem to have been written in 1653; the two long Cromwell poems belong to 1654 and 1658; and the elegant 'On Mr. Milton's *Paradise Lost*' comes in 1674, *after* Marvell's longest political satire, 'The Last Instructions to a Painter' and just before the 'Statue poems'—assuming that Marvell wrote the latter. Unless we can learn a great deal more about the composition and dating of Marvell's poems than it seems likely we ever shall, any attempt to present a precisely detailed account of Marvell's psychological or aesthetic development is doomed to depend on more than usually random hunches or abstracting fictions.

If the prevalent notions about seventeenth-century literary history and Marvell's development have not always proved helpful, the attempts to place Marvell in a specific 'school' of poetry have also occasionally misled or perplexed. A student who has learned that Marvell belongs to the 'School of Donne' may be disconcerted when he discovers Marvell's concern for euphony, his usual rejection of impatient or impassioned speakers, and his preference for simple metrical schemes and Jonsonian diction. If he has learned that Marvell was a 'Metaphysical Poet' and that 'Metaphysical Poets' were either Anglo or Roman Catholic, what can he make of Marvell's open hostility to both? In his effort to preserve the teaching that 'Metaphysical Poets' were partisans of Charles and enemies of Cromwell, a bright student may try to read 'An Horatian Ode' as a poem that expresses primary allegiance to Charles, but what can he do with the other two Cromwell poems?

If his primary aim is really to understand—and to enjoy—Marvell's poems, he might abandon, at least temporarily, the attempt to fit them into historical or critical categories and pay more attention to the differing sorts of audiences that, throughout his career, Marvell seems to have had in mind for the poems and also to the methods of argument and the rhetorical structures that he developed within them.

ii

Along with the unusually 'private' poems, Marvell wrote a number of semi-private ones, poems intended directly for specific readers but not for publication. Both 'Upon the Hill and Grove at Bilbrough' and 'Upon Appleton House' are subtitled, the first 'To the Lord Fairfax' and the second 'To my Lord Fairfax.' (The 'my' correctly indicates the greater degree of intimacy of the second.) Although neither poem addresses Fairfax openly, each is obviously written for his eyes as well as in his honour. Yet each seems much more 'private' than the usual seventeenth-century poem addressed to a famous public man; both of them reflect, I believe, Marvell's special status as a member of the household (the tutor of Fairfax's daughter), and although one can imagine either the poet's or Fairfax's sharing them privately with friends, I do not think one can imagine either's having them published. Perhaps this special semi-private quality partly accounts for the apparent freedom and fancifulness of 'Upon Appleton House,' the most interesting long poem that I know between *The Faerie Queene* and *Paradise Lost*. 'Music's Empire,' with what seems the compliment in its final lines to Fairfax, probably belongs roughly to the same group, and the sung pastoral dialogues that Marvell wrote for the marriage of Cromwell's daughter also have a tone of personal commendation and seem created for a larger but still a semi-private audience.[3] The original version of 'On the Victory obtained by Blake' seems intended privately for the eyes of Cromwell. It may just be possible that 'An Horatian Ode,' with its dramatic shift to direct address in line 113 ('But thou the Wars and Fortunes Son / March indefatigably on'), may also be conceived as a semi-private commendation to Cromwell; if so, the poem is even more daring than most scholars and critics have imagined.

A much less unusual group of poems is formed by the public encomiums which Marvell wrote, in his own person and with his name attached, for publication in volumes by or in honour of the men he praised. They include the poem to Lovelace, Marvell's contribution to the volume on the death of Lord Hastings, the one on *Paradise Lost*, and the one 'To his Worthy Friend Doctor Witty upon his Translation of the Popular Errors.' The latter contains some of Marvell's sharpest literary criticism. Its description of the faults of translators should be better known that it is:

> Some in this task
> Take off the cypress veil, but leave a mask,

Changing the Latin, but do more obscure
That sense in English which was bright and pure.
So of translators they are authors grown,
For ill translators make the book their own.
Others do strive with words and forcèd phrase
To add such lustre, and so many rays,
That but to make the vessel shining, they
Much of the precious metal rub away.
He is translation's thief that addeth more,
As much as he that taketh from the store
Of that first author. Here he maketh blots
That mends; and added beauties are but spots.

Although the genre is a conventional one, there is nothing tamely conventional about Marvell's handling of it. I shall return to the *Paradise Lost* poem.

The least read and probably the most poorly read of Marvell's poems today are the fully public ones which Marvell wrote for anonymous publication and with which he meant to influence public opinion. They include 'The Character of Holland,' 'The First Anniversary of the Government under O. C.,' and the satires of the Restoration. Related to them if not actually included are 'An Horatian Ode,' 'Tom May's Death,' and 'On the Victory obtained by Blake.' Marvell obviously intended 'A Peom upon the Death of O. C.' to be a fully political poem, but I think it fails of his intention precisely because it presents the poet's sorrow and near despair so frankly that it undercuts its final attempt to build political support for Richard Cromwell. The later satires, both the few about which we can feel fairly sure and the many which were attributed to him, reflect the fact that after his election to Parliament in 1659, Marvell devoted his major energies to public matters—and numbers of people knew it. I do not find it at all self-evident that we always have the right to regret it when a poet becomes so concerned with public affairs that he either devotes his poetry to them or gives it up. Milton's is, of course, one of the most startling examples; but even had Milton died before completing *Paradise Lost*, I think we should have had no just right (though excuse enough) to lament the political pamphlets and the Latin Secretaryship. There was hardly for Milton a possible choice between either the poetry or the public career, since he believed that he could not write heroic poetry unless he was willing to sacrifice his private ambition when he thought public duty required him to do so. In Marvell's case, it is almost impossible to imagine a poet so intelligent, so witty, and so constant in his attendance on the parliaments of Charles II who could resist the promise—and the satisfactions—of verse satire.

Some readers' difficulties with Marvell's political poetry may stem from a critical assumption quite widespread a few years ago that the most 'mature' (and therefore literarily desirable) human attitude is an ironic embracement of all contradictory impulses—a condition of complete paralysis costing not less than everything. One can certainly understand, too, the temptation in our age to identify the serious poet as precisely the person who is not selling anything, and to assume that any poet must compromise his private standards if he attempts to influence public action. Still, such notions are seriously anachronistic; moreover, they are not likely to prove very helpful for our reading of most panegyrics and satires. Probably making for more immediate difficulties with Marvell's poetry is the prevalence among scholars and critics of a sentimental royalism. (Americans are often particularly subject to it: there are supposedly more chapels dedicated to Blessed Charles King and Martyr

in the state of Texas than in all the British Isles.) Many
sensitive and learned readers would rather not be reminded
of Marvell's poems in praise of Cromwell, and some of
them have spent a good deal of ingenuity on attempts to
read 'An Horatian Ode' as a covertly Cavalier poem. A
number have accepted the attribution to Marvell of the
blood-thirstily royalist 'An Elegy upon the Death of my
Lord Francis Villiers,' a poem which it seems most
unlikely that Marvell wrote.[4]

John M. Wallace's recent volume, *Destiny His Choice*:
The Loyalism of Andrew Marvell,[5] contains some of the
most interesting recent pages on the political poems.
Rather than beginning with the question, 'What does the
poem mean to me, privately?' Wallace has tended to ask
two other questions, 'What was the poem's immediate
political context?' and 'What is the poem's rhetorical
structure?' Among other things, his readings demonstrate
that the range of possible political positions at any one
moment in Marvell's career was a good deal wider than
modern readers are likely to assume. I am indebted to
Mr Wallace in my following attempt to sketch the
workings of two of those poems, 'The First Anniversary
of the Government under O. C.' and 'The Last Instructions to a Painter,' Marvell's longest and most sustained
examples of political celebration and political satire. (The
latter is also one of the few Restoration satires of which
the attribution to Marvell has never been seriously
questioned.) Both poems show that Marvell was an intelligent and witty poet who knew what he was doing and
thoroughly enjoyed doing it. In neither is there any
ambiguity at all about the central attitudes: the first
prasies Cromwell as a 'Prince' who has surpassed all
former and present kings and has miraculously created a

strong and just England out of what had been remarkably near chaos; the second satirizes unmercifully the political events and personalities of 1666-67, and argues that Charles II must summon new advisers if he and England are to survive. Readers interested in history and in Marvell will probably be interested in those arguments in themselves. But the literary effectiveness of the poems depends chiefly on how the positions are managed: whether we are shown and made to feel the reality, in the first poem, of a governor and a government worthy of being preserved; and, in the second, of a public situation so hopelessly venal and inefficient, that, while we laugh, we recognize with the poet that it must be changed.

'The First Anniversary,' written for December of 1654 and published anonymously shortly thereafter, begins with the contrast between the usual triumph of time over mortal man and the fate of Cromwell:

> Like the vain curlings of the watery maze,
> Which in smooth streams a sinking weight does raise;
> So Man, declining always, disappears
> In the weak circles of increasing years;
> And his short tumults of themselves compose,
> While flowing time above his head does close.
>   *Cromwell* alone with greater vigour runs,
> (Sun-like) the stages of succeeding suns:
> And still the day which he doth next restore,
> Is the just wonder of the day before.
> *Cromwell* alone doth with new lustre spring,
> And shines the jewel of the yearly ring.

The first section of the poem celebrates what Cromwell is and what he has done. What we have thought of him before is, supposedly, irrelevant: the imaginatively contrasted paragraphs proceed 'objectively' in the third person. In the rapid sequence of witty, mythic images of Cromwell (as the sun who triumphs over time, as the miraculous musician-architect who surpasses Amphion, as the Archimedes who has found a place for his foot and 'hurls' the world about him), Marvell created a vision of a dynamic force, both part of and superior to ordinary nature, which cannot fail to interest his readers. The section ends with the wish that the benighted Princes would recognize Cromwell as the leader capable of achieving 'The Great Designs kept for the Latter Days.'

At this point the objective narration ceases with an apostrophe to the 'Unhappy Princes.' Then the speculations of the 'I' create the 'we' for the rest of the poem:

> Hence oft *I* think if in some happy hour
> High Grace should meet in one with highest pow'r,
> And then a seasonable people still,
> Should bend to his, as he to Heaven's will,
> What *we* might hope. . . .   (ll. 131-35; my italics)

But although we can know of the 'great designs,' we cannot know of their times: ''tis the most which we determine can, / if these the Times, then this must be the Man.'

Only after the 'objective' description of Cromwell and his creation, and after the personal statement which anticipates and re-directs the arguments of the Millenerian opposition in such a way that 'we' must join, does the poem turn to address Cromwell directly: 'And thou, great Cromwell. . . .' The implications of the 'thou' and the new 'we' are largely sustained in the rhetorical inventions which move us swiftly to the conclusion. Despite Cromwell's birth, virtue, and miraculous escapes from death, 'Our sins endanger, and shall one day kill' him. His recent coaching accident provides the evidence. At the thought of his possible death there, 'We only mourned ourselves,' for Cromwell, like Elijah, would have ascended. Cromwell had already given up 'all delight of life' when he became 'the headstrong people's charioteer': he was the cloud which brought plenty to the thirsty land, the Gideon who conquered and yet refused to be 'Lord,' the olive which only 'in just time didst awe' 'Th' ambitious shrubs.' The simile of the 'lusty mate' who saved the ship of state when the 'artless' Barebones parliamentarians were about to wreck it provides the occasion for the poem's definition of freedom and of Cromwell as the Father:

> 'Tis not a freedom, that where all command;
> Nor tyranny, where one doth them withstand:
> But who of both the bound'r'es knows to lay
> Him as their Father must the State obey.   (ll. 279-82)

Cromwell is the Noah who has survived the Flood and established a new world. The 'Chammish issue' have hoped he would be killed, but Cromwell, 'returning yet alive / Does with himself all that is good revive.' At the thought of his death, we were like the first man who, experiencing the first sunset and night, followed the fallen sun in despair: 'When straight the sun behind him he descried, / Smiling serenely from the further side.' The hostile princes, startled by that sun, give the ultimate praise to the revived nation and to the might of the English navy, but it is Cromwell, the 'soul' of that nation, whom they fear most. When the single speaker interrupts their unwilling praise, he addresses Cromwell at last as 'great Prince.' Yet, although that title may have been intended to have profound political significance outside the poem, within it, it seems almost incidental, since the poem itself has 'proved' that as sun, architect, musician, creator, prophet, soldier, great captain, father, day, star, and soul of the nation, Cromwell *is* greater far 'Then ought below, or yet abouve a King.' If the hostile monarchs want him to take the title of king only to prove his common mortality with them, then we, of course, do not wish it. Cromwell is semi-deified and the great anniversary fully celebrated; yet time has not stopped. The poet will no longer contend for the prize of praising Cromwell properly *while* Cromwell raises his 'venerable' head 'As far above their malice as my praise,' and while 'the *Angel* of our Commonweal, / Troubling the waters, yearly mak'st them heal.' The conclusion both completes the praise and makes clearly evident the relation of this anniversary to the uncertain future, when, with the ultimate disturbance of the waters by his death, Cromwell will no longer be living to heal them. Politically, the poem not only praises Cromwell and rallies support for him, but it also emphasizes the pressing importance of some solution to the problem of the succession.

'Upon the First Anniversary' can still be remarkably effective as a whole. 'The Last Instructions to a Painter' is likely as a whole to remain the preserve of the specialists. Written in the early fall of 1667, it surveys the political events and Court scandals of the preceding year so fully (in almost a thousand lines) that it inevitably has some of the obscurity of any detailed annal centuries later, when the personalities and the events are forgotten. Yet the surprising thing about the poem is not how much of it may seem dead, but how much, even at the most cursory reading, still seems alive.

Only the year before, in 1666, Edmund Waller had published 'Instructions to a Painter, For the Drawing of the Posture and Progress of His Majesty's Forces at Sea, Under the command of His Highness Royal, Together with the Battle and Victory obtained over the Dutch, June 3, 1665.' He thereby became, quite unintentionally, the English father of an entire satirical genre. For in his fulsome praise of the Duke of York for the 'great victory' of Lowestoft, Waller failed to mention the facts that after the battle the Dutch fleet was allowed to escape because the Duke was taking a nap and that subsequent events were not generally considered cause for English rejoicing. The satirical possibilities were seized upon by a number of writers. Despite its title, Marvell's contribution to the genre[6] was by no means the last of the 'Advice to a Painter' poems which derived from Waller panegyric, but it is the best.

Marvell's 'Instructions' should discourage the painter from the start. No one medium will serve to paint the monstrous 'Confusion, folly, treach'ry, fear, neglect' which characterize 'Our Lady State':

> After two sittings, now our *Lady State*,
> To end her picture, does the third time wait.
> But ere thou fall'st to work, first *Painter* see
> It ben't too slight grown, or too hard for thee.
> Canst thou paint without Colours? Then 'tis right:
> For so we too without a fleet can fight.
> Or canst thou daub a sign-post, and that ill?
> 'Twill suit our great debauch and little skill.
> Or hast thou mark't how antique Masters limn
> The alley roof, with snuff of candle dimn,
> Sketching in shady smoke prodigious tools?
> 'Twill serve this race of Drunkards, Pimps, and Fools.
> But if to match our crimes thy skill presumes,
> As th' *Indians*, draw our luxury in plumes.
> Or if to core out our compendious Fame,
> With *Hook* then, through the microscope take aim. . . .
>
> (ll. 1-16)

Without such resources, the painter shall 'oft' curse his 'guiltless pencil' and 'Stamp on' his 'Pallet'; and these gestures of rage may prove the most effective strokes of all:

> So may'st thou perfect, by a lucky blow,
> What all thy softest touches cannot do.   (ll. 27-28)

For the task at hand the poet and painter will need the resources of savage indignation as well as of artful disdain.

The poet invites the painter to paint a number of horrendous portraits; he may also paint a trick-track board (with the dice deciding fate) as an image of the House of Commons, and a large battle-piece to represent the debate over the Excise Bill. But most of the time the painter must 'rest' and observe 'With what small arts the public game they play'; he cannot possibly paint a single comprehensive canvas since 'Our Lady State' at this time has neither centre nor coherence. The poet finally bids the painter adieu; Charles, now that he has dismissed Clarendon, will surely become both poet and painter and sit for himself. The envoy begs Charles to dismiss the false courtiers who, 'where all England serves, themselves would reign,' to summon a true Court, and to 'rule without a Guard.' With the idea of a restoration of natural order, an 'ideal' poem and picture become again possible.

In the meantime, there is the problem of this poem: how *does* one construct an admonitory picture of chaos?[7] Historical 'order' may be far from ideal, but at least it exists; and Marvell, after his portraits of St. Albans, the Duchess of York, and the Countess Castlemaine (all sexually depraved and all with past or future designs upon the crown), turns largely to episodic narrative of the parliamentary, military, and diplomatic events: the struggle over the Excise, which is neither a decent back-

gammon game nor a proper battle; the absurd and self-
righteous diplomacy with the Dutch and French; the
ironic pastoral triumph of de Ruyter and the Dutch fleet
as they rape the Thames and Medway; the one example
of mythic integrity and suffering in the death of Douglas,
the 'Valiant Scot'; the renewed intrigue with the prospect
of peace. But with all the variety and disorder, the concept of sovereignty—the poem's 'picture' of those who
really rule, or wish to rule, or attempt or pretend to rule—
provides more unity than we at first suspect. It is Clarendon who 'Reigns in his new palace' and 'sits in State
Divine' after the House is prorogued; it is Louis and the
Dutch who possess real civil and military power; it is de
Ruyter who truly rules the ocean, the English rivers, and
later the English navy (the gallants, who came 'To be
spectators safe of the *new Play*,' flee in comic disorder
when the dramatic issues of sovereignty become actual);
it is 'brave Douglas' who will rule in legend as hero—the
Court can only coin a new farthing with the image of the
Duchess of Richmond as Britannia 'ruling the *four Seas*';
the Court wishes to isolate Parliament from any share
in ruling, and a corrupt Speaker rules Parliament; it is
Charles who must, as King *in* Parliament, begin to rule.

And throughout the poem is Marvell's wit. The Court
party chose Peter Pett, Commissioner of the Navy at
Chatham, as the scapegoat for the entire naval disaster;
we do not have to know anything about the historical
realities to respond to those sixteen lines for which *Pett*
supplies the rhymes and to delight in the climactic
unmasking of the absurdity:

> Who all our ships exposed in Chatham's net?
> Who should it be but the *Phanatic Pett*.

> *Pett*, the sea architect, in making ships,
> Was the first cause of all these naval slips:
> Had he not built, none of these faults had bin;
> If no Creation, there had been no Sin.   (ll. 783-88)

It was an inspiration to imagine that if, during the year, Charles II had been visited by a nude female vision of distressed England or the Peace, his response would have been erotic rather than political; yet in his Envoy to Charles, Marvell makes one of the last moving appeals to the older idea of the English royal commonwealth.

If we are to read most of Marvell's political poems intelligently and with pleasure, we need to know more than we do. But even a glance at 'The First Anniversary' and 'The Last Instructions' suggests a number of points which scholars and critics might keep in mind while they attempt to increase our knowledge. Marvell used and mastered more than one style. When he wrote occasional poems, he was aware of a potential public audience and of immediate political possibilities. (He would surely have considered the unintentional admission into either a panegyric or a satire of an individual poet's private misgivings an example not of 'honesty' but of incompetence.) And he seems to have realized that political poems, like other poems, are less immediately effective and less ultimately interesting if the poet assumes that he is merely voicing common sentiment, formulated before his poem is written—or read. Whether panegyrist or satirist, the poet must appropriate, undermine, or destroy those visions and attitudes in the external world which oppose or differ from the central visions and judgements of his poem.

If we recognize these things, the other political and quasi-political poems may become less problematic and more interesting. We may be able to read 'The Character

175

of Holland' as a cheerful libel on the Dutch people and culture, more humane in its playful exaggeration and a great deal funnier than the wartime propaganda we are used to. We may see that 'On the Victory obtained by Blake,' in the midst of its rhetorical congratulations, takes full advantage of the prophetic possibilities offered by the fact that the Spanish gold (instrument of oppression and future wars) was sent to the bottom of the sea in the Canary Islands—a setting, like the Bermudas, which offered an Edenic image of the political possibilities ahead for Cromwell and England. We might find Shake-spearean analogies for 'An Horatian Ode' in *Richard II* and *Henry IV* rather than in *Macbeth*, and see the Charles of the poem as tragic because, like Richard, he only achieves nobility and fully acts his role as king when he forfeits his crown and his life to a 'greater Spirit.' And we might consider the possibility that Marvell makes the ghost of Ben Jonson so denunciatory in 'Tom May's Death,' not because of Marvell's fervent royalism, but because, whatever the politics, he despised the pettiness, the venality, the hypocrisy, and the broken faith that he thought May had shown.[8] In attempting to judge the authenticity of the later satires, we might hold on to the fact that Marvell is rarely dull or awkward; but we might not rule out the possibility that, when political conditions become desperate and his verse had to go underground, a poet of his skill *could* have used the popular, galloping accentual verse for rough and devas-tating effects.

When we read Marvell's political writings, we get an impression of integrity that implies more than the poet's mastery of rhetoric. Marvell was committed to the great-ness of England and to freedom of conscience, and he was seriously engaged with the major political personalities as well as issues of his time. Except for the poems on the birth of Princess Anne (written when he was sixteen), Marvell never wrote a poem to Charles I which praised him; nor did he ever denigrate him: even in the most violent of the later satires, he presented that Charles as primarily benighted and betrayed by his own supporters rather than as the betrayer. Marvell did not welcome Charles II with a panegyric after composing a funeral ode for Cromwell, nor during his long career in Restoration politics did he ever slander the Cromwell he had so much praised. Except for the pleading conclusion of 'The Last Instructions,' he never wrote anything resembling panegyric verse to Charles II. In a century when the shifts of most poets who attempted political poetry are occasionally embarrassing to their admirers, Marvell's principles and practice remained remarkably consistent.

Marvell's political maturity occurred during a revolution and a counter-revolution. Such times make simple traditionalism and constitutionalism intellectually impossible: they pose the fearful questions about what could and should happen when the traditions contradict each other, when the constitutions break down. One can heartily agree that it is probably better to have no interesting political poems than to experience such times, and still recognize that the possibility or reality or memory of such occasions is likely, along with the brutal, to give rise to the most interesting political poetry. For if the poet writes anything beyond battle cries and curses, such times prevent his relapsing thoughtlessly into the formulae of conventional wisdom. He must re-examine his inheritance and the present and create an image of order which, however much it owes to the past, is something new.

iii

Although he continued until the year of his death to write his witty prose attacks on various men and subjects associated with religious intolerance and strict Calvinist determinism, Marvell seems to have written his last verse satire in 1675. Just the year before, he published 'On Mr. Milton's *Paradise Lost*' as prefatory to the second edition. Marvell's poem is, I think the only rival of Carew's Elegy on Donne as the seventeenth-century poem which most effectively turns literary criticism into poetry; it dramatizes beautifully the process by which private hesitancies and discriminations can be transformed into clear and powerful public judgements.

Marvell's association with Milton had been long: he had admired and used Milton's early verse soon after it was published; Milton had recommended him as his assistant as Latin Secretary; and the two men had become friends. According to contemporary report, Marvell helped save Milton's life after the Restoration, and he defended him both in the House of Commons and in print. With the publication of *Paradise Lost*, Marvell may have recognized that, despite his use of Jonson's lyrics in his earlier poems, Milton was the first major poet after Donne and Jonson who was not primarily an heir of either. If Milton had a single important English ancestor, it was, of course, Spenser. Good classicist that Marvell was (I sometimes think of him as playing Horace to Milton's Vergil), Marvell must have particularly responded to the way in which for the first time a man of his own world had successfully undertaken a role not merely as an imitator but as a competitor of the ancient epic poets.

Marvell lets no trace of personal intimacy show in his

178

poem, but, properly for its occasion, makes it a fully public encomium. He begins with three paragraphs (totalling 22 lines) concerning his initial suspicions of, and fears for, *Paradise Lost*. First, the vast subject (and Marvell's summary of it is splendid) made him fear that 'sacred truths' might be 'ruined' 'to fable and old song,' and even that Milton may have intended so 'overwhelming' 'the world' as revenge for his blindness. Then, acknowledging the poet's admirable intentions, he feared that he might not succeed in fulfilling them, but would only 'perplex' or 'render vain' religious events and truths. And even if Milton succeeded, his example might lead others to imitate him who would cheapen the sacred subjects. (Here, a particular shaft is aimed at Marvell's *bête noire*, John Dryden, and his plan for *The State of Innocence*.)

Only after describing the doubts and fears does the poet address Milton directly and resolve the misgivings (in reverse order) with three more paragraphs summarizing the evidence of Milton's poem: it is so good as to defy imitators; its majesty preserves both the sacred truths and the poet; it owes its inspiration not to revenge (like Samson's) but to Heaven's consolatory inspiration (like Tiresias'). These paragraphs of unequal length, like the first three, total 22 lines: characteristically, underneath the apparent casualness the balance is precise:

> Pardon me, Mighty Poet, nor despise
> My causeless, yet not impious, surmise.
> But I am now convinced, and none will dare
> Within thy labours to pretend a share.
> Thou hast not missed one thought that could be fit,
> And all that was improper dost omit:
> So that no room is here for writers left,
> But to detect their ignorance or theft.

> That Majesty which through thy work doth reign
> Draws the devout, deterring the profane.
> And things divine thou treatst of in such state
> As them preserves, and thee, inviolate.
> At once delight and horrour on us seize,
> Thou singst with so much gravity and ease;
> And above humane flight dost soar aloft,
> With plume so strong, so equal, and so soft.
> The bird named from that Paradise you sing
> So never flags, but always keeps on wing.
> Where couldst thou words of such a compass find?
> Whence furnish such a vast expense of mind?
> Just Heav'n thee, like Tiresias, to requite,
> Rewards with prophecy thy loss of sight.   (ll. 23-44)

I doubt that Marvell's description of the 'majesty' of *Paradise Lost* has ever been bettered. Then, separating his own discourse from the described grandeur of Milton's, Marvell adds a stylish coda, focusing on the chief technical novelty of the poem (the non-dramatic blank verse) and including another swat at Dryden and a distinction between the poems which need rhyme and those which do not:

> Well mightst thou scorn thy readers to allure
> With tinkling rhyme, of thy own sense secure;
> While the *Town-Bays* writes all the while and spells,
> And like a pack-horse tires without his bells:
> Their fancies like our bushy-points appear;
> The poets tag them, we for fashion wear.
> I too transported by the mode offend,
> And while I meant to *praise* thee, must *commend*.
> Thy verse created like thy theme sublime,
> In Number, Weight, and Measure, needs not rhyme.

Marvell clearly recognized and admired the miracle of *Paradise Lost*, but, except in a few lines, he did not imitate it. Perhaps he recognized that Milton's combination of blank verse and high style, divorced from greatness of subject and greatness of spirit, was likely to result merely in windiness or bombast. And Marvell, ostentatiously staying with the couplets that had served him so well, correctly reflected the mode of 1674 and anticipated the most promising manner of the immediate future. The best poets of the next half-century would prove to be only more remote heirs of Jonson as they further developed a verse that, subjecting private taste to rational examination, moves towards a balanced and witty poetry of public judgement.

NOTES TO CHAPTER I

1. *George Herbert: His Religion and Art* (London and Cambridge, Mass., 1954), pp. 203-04.

2. (Oxford, 2nd ed., 1962), pp. 76-179.

3. *Elizabethan Taste* (London, 1963), pp. 317-38.

4. Quoted by Buxton, *Elizabethan Taste*, pp. 317-18.

5. *The Satires, Epigrams and Verse Letters* (Oxford, 1967), p. 52.

6. 'Confined Love.' The other poem is 'Break of Day.'

7. John Donne, *The Elegies and The Songs and Sonnets* (Oxford, 1965), p. xvii.

8. 'Euclia's Hymn' from *Love's Triumph through Callipolis, Ben Jonson*, ed. C. H. Herford and Percy and Evelyn Simpson, VII (Oxford, 1941), 740.

9. Cf. Helen Gardner's remarks in her edition of *The Divine Poems* (Oxford, 1952), pp. xv-xvii.

10. Letter to Sir Robert Carr in 1625, quoted by Gardner, *The Elegies and The Songs and Sonnets*, p. xviii.

11. Donne's poem is also more impressive than another of Jonson's efforts for the same occasion, *The Irish Masque at Court*.

12. Louis Martz, *The Poetry of Meditation* (New Haven and London, 2nd ed., 1962), pp. 211-48; cf. also George Williamson's 'The Design of Donne's *Anniversaries*,' '*Modern Philogy*,' LX (1963), 183-91.

13. *English Literature in the Earlier Seventeenth Century*, p. 107.

NOTES TO CHAPTER II

1. For Herrick's life see L. C. Martin's biographical sketch in his edition of *The Poetical Works* (Oxford, 1956), pp. xi-xvii.

2. Cf. Bush, *English Literature in the Earlier Seventeenth Century*, p. 116.

3. See Martin's Commentary, *The Poetical Works*, pp. 498-584.

4. I believe I owe the point to Mr Gene Koppel.

5. I am indebted to Cleanth Brooks' analysis of the poem in *The Well Wrought Urn* (New York, 1947), pp. 67-75.

6. For Carew's life see Rhodes Dunlap's Introduction to his edition of *The Poems* (Oxford, 1949), pp. xiii-xlv.

7. See Rufus A. Blanshard's 'Thomas Carew and the Cavalier Poets,' *Transactions of the Wisconsin Academy of Science, Arts and Letters*, XLIII (1954), 97-105 and his 'Carew and Jonson,' '*Studies in Philology*,' LII (1955), 195-211.

8. See Dunlap's note, *The Poems*, p. 246.

9. Introduction to Ezra Pound's *Selected Poems* (London, 1933), p. xviii.

10. See Dunlap's note on the masque, *The Poems*, pp. 273-77.

NOTES TO CHAPTER III

1. For King's biography see Margaret Crum's Introduction to her edition of *The Poems* (Oxford, 1965), pp. 1-27.

2. *English Literature in the Earlier Seventeenth Century*, p. 12.

3. *The Poems*, p. 5. For Westminster's probable influence on King's verse, see pp. 29-30.

4. Crum, *The Poems*, p. 1, quotes Walton's account.

5. *English Literature in the Earlier Seventeenth Century*, p. 162.

6. *The Poems*, pp. 10, 247-48.

7. 'An Elegy upon the immature loss of the most virtuous Lady Ann Rich,' ll. 71-72.

8. For the stanza and other variations see *Minor Poets of the Caroline Period*, ed. George Saintsbury, III (Oxford, 1921), 236-37; cf. Crum, Appendix III, *The Poems*, pp. 254-55.

9. For Herbert's biography see F. E. Hutchinson's splendid edition of *The Works* (Oxford, rev. ed., 1954), pp. xxi-xxxix.

10. *The Lives* (London: World's Classics, 1927), p. 275.

11. See Helen Gardner's Appendix G in Donne, *The Divine Poems*, pp. 138-47.

12. 'The Titles of Donne's Poems,' *Friendship's Garland: Essays Presented to Mario Praz on His Seventieth Birthday*, ed. Vittorio Gabrieli (Rome, 1966), I, 190-91.

NOTES

13. *Texts & Pretexts* (New York, 1933), p. 164.

14. See Hutchinson's note, *The Works*, pp. 483-84.

15. *The Lives*, p. 314.

16. Albert McHarg Hayes, 'Counterpoint in Herbert,' '*Studies in Philology*,' XXXV (1938), 56.

17. See Gene H. Koretz, 'The Rhyme Scheme in Herbert's "Man",' '*Notes and Queries*,' n.s., III (1956), 144-46.

NOTES TO CHAPTER IV

1. Richard Crashaw, *The Poems, English, Latin and Greek* ed. L. C. Martin (Oxford, 2nd ed., 1957), pp. 75-77.

2. See Austin Warren, *Richard Crashaw: A Study in Baroque Sensibility* (Ann Arbor, 1957), p. 220.

3. *Richard Crashaw*, p. 112.

4. *Richard Crashaw*, pp. 127-28.

5. See Martin's Commentary, *The Works*, p. 433.

6. *English Literature in the Earlier Seventeenth Century*, p. 147.

7. ii. 323-45.

8. Cf. Warren, *Richard Crashaw*, pp. 109-10.

9. The Nativity Hymn, *Carmen Deo Nostro* version (1652), ll. 46-47.

10. *English Literature in the Earlier Seventeenth Century*, p. 150.

11. For Vaughan's life see F. E. Hutchinson, *Henry Vaughan: A Life and Interpretation* (Oxford, 1947).

12. *The Works of Henry Vaughan*, ed. L. C. Martin (Oxford, 2nd ed., 1957), p. 2.

13. *The Works*, p. 689.

14. p. 694.

15. p. 695.

16. p. 249.

17. pp. 388, 391.

18. *Henry Vaughan*, pp. 102-03.

19. See Ross Garner, *Henry Vaughan: Experience and the Tradition* (Chicago, 1959), *passim*.

20. 'We are safe in relating Vaughan's fondness for the word *white*, as an epithet for all he values most, to the rich connotations of the Welsh word *gwyn* which signifies not only white but fair, happy, holy, blessed. There is no more frequent epithet in Welsh poetry, it is the word which introduces each of the Beatitudes in the Sermon on the Mount, and a Welsh word for Paradise is *gwynfyd*, the white world.'—*Henry Vaughan*, p. 162. Hutchinson's entire chapter, 'Henry Vaughan, Silurist', pp. 156-64, is illuminating concerning the Welsh elements in the verse.

21. According to my recollection of a conversation with F. O. Matthiessen in 1950.

22. In *The Flaming Heart* (New York, 1958), pp. 204-63.

NOTES TO CHAPTER V

1. London, 1966.

2. *The Art of Marvell's Poetry*, p. 197.

3. I have attempted a brief sketch of the way the poem works in the Introduction to my edition of *Marvell: Selected Poems* (New York, 1961), pp. 17-25. M. J. K. O'Loughlin has published an interesting essay on the poem in *Andrew Marvell: A Collection of Critical Essays*, ed. George deF. Lord (Englewood Cliffs, N.J., 1968), pp. 120-42. Rosalie Colie's forthcoming *My Echoing Song* will contain a splendidly comprehensive account of 'Upon Appleton House.'

4. For an account of early responses to the poem, see Pierre Legouis, *Andrew Marvell: Poet, Puritan, Patriot* (Oxford, 1965), pp. 233-37.

5. Originally published in *Essays in Criticism* (1952), it is now conveniently available in *Seventeenth-Century English Poetry: Modern Essays in Criticism*, ed. William R. Keast (New York, 1962), pp. 290-304. In 'Marvell Transprosed,' *Encounter*, XXVI (1966), 77-84, Kermode attacked modern excesses in the reading of Marvell's poetry but did not discuss 'The Garden' specifically.

NOTES

In the Introduction and extensive annotations of his *Andrew Marvell: Selected Poetry* (New York and London, 1967), Kermode is informative, suggestive, and sensible about 'The Garden.'

6. *Hortus* is available in an edition of Marvell's Latin poetry with English translations *en face*: William A. McQueen and Kiffin A. Rockwell, *The Latin Poetry of Andrew Marvell* (Chapel Hill, 1964), pp. 20-27. Grierson and the most recent editors are probably correct in suggesting that *Hortus* is an earlier version of 'The Garden' that may well be complete—despite the *Desunt multa* after l. 48 in the 1681 *Miscellaneous Poems*. A full study of the poem in its own right is still needed. The most important formal relations between the two poems are roughly as follows: The first 6 lines of *Hortus* correspond to stanza i of 'The Garden'; the next 13 lines to stanza ii; the next 12 to stanza iii; and the following 17 lines are a much expanded version of stanza iv. Nothing in *Hortus* truly corresponds to stanzas v-viii, but the last 10 lines of the Latin poem are very close to the last stanza of 'The Garden.' The 'centre' of the Latin poem is the tranformation of sexual desire, both for the speaker and the gods, into the love of the trees and the reed. Perhaps *Hortus is* a playfully exaggerated poem in the 'anti-genre of the naturalist paradise,' as Kermode in his earlier essay suggested 'The Garden' was. But stanzas v-vii give 'The Garden' a different centre. (Cf. George Williamson, 'Marvell's "Hortus" and "Garden",' *Milton & Others* [London, 1965], pp. 140-49).

7. *Municipem servate novum, votoque potitum,* | *Frondosae Cives optate in florea Regna* (ll. 14-15).

8. The use of *teneo* in *Hortus* rather than 'found' seems to anticipate the amorousness that is to come: *Alma Quies, teneo te!* & *te Germana Quietis* | *Simplicitas!*

9. McQueen and Rockwell's translation of line 40.

10. Geoffrey H. Hartman's 'Marvell, St. Paul, and the Body of Hope,' *ELH*, XXXI (1964), 175-94, strikes me as one of the most interesting recent essays concerning the poem; but I think the author is wrong to read it as if the behaviour of the fruits was supposed to be 'alarming.' Surely the image here is of a sublimated sexual Cockaigne—where the fish jump into the net and honey drops from trees.

11. Stanza viii states that it is like Eden was before there was any possibility of sinning.

187

12. Hartman misses the separation. He writes (p. 184): 'The picture of the soul in VII stands over against its previous evocations. Instead of being insnared (as in V) it here does its own snaring . . . The soul will not leave the garden by a premature ecstasy, as in VI. . . .' But the soul is not described in stanzas v and vi.

13. I am not satisfied with my understanding of ll. 49-50 ('Here at the foundtain's sliding foot, / Or at some fruit-tree's mossy root'), but I am convinced that we are doing violence to the poem if we smuggle any literal baptismal font or Tree of Knowledge into them. To leave the 'body's vest' at 'Some fruit-tree's mossy root' would seem to place the soul's ecstasy as precisely simultaneous with the sublimated sensuality and implied fertility of the body's ecstasy in stanza v ('Ripe apples drop about my head'); and the grass *could* be 'at the fountain's sliding foot,' too. As Professor Kermode suggested (p. 302), the fountain is probably 'an easily accessible emblem of purity'; it may also be associated with fertility, particularly the fertility of the mind, 'that ocean' which has just been described. The chief point, as I understand it, is that the place where the body is 'cast aside' by the soul does not matter so long as it is innocent, pleasant, and capable of association with the ecstasies of body and mind.

NOTES TO CHAPTER VI

1. See H. M. Margoliouth's note in *The Poems and Letters of Andrew Marvell* (Oxford, 2nd ed., 1952), I, xiii.

2. For the latter, see Ann E. Berthoff, 'The Allegorical Metaphor: Marvell's "The Definition of Love," ' '*Reveiw of English Studies,*' XVIII' (1966), 16-29.

3. The other pastoral dialogues may also have been conceived for public musical performances. William Lawes (d. 1645), John Gamble, and Matthew Locke all set 'A Dialogue between Thrysis and Dorinda.' Almost anyone who listens to Locke's setting (available on Westminster Records XWN-19082) will be struck by the different effects (and the different questions one asks) when one hears that poem as a musical performance rather than as a 'privately' written dialogue.

4. Margoliouth printed the poem in an Appendix with a long note by C. H. Wilkinson pressing its claims (I, 329, 334), but he did not state his own acceptance of the attribution. A single copy of the poem was left by George Clarke (1660-1736) to the Library of Worcester College, Oxford, and the donor's manuscript notation, 'by Andrew Marvell,' is the sole evidence for attribution. Although Clarke was a careful collector whose attributions are valuable for works of the late seventeenth and eighteenth centuries, there seems to be no other case in which they are at all significant for works written before his birth in 1660. I find it difficult to believe that the same poet could have written the poem on Lovelace in February of 1648 and the poem on Hastings in June of 1649 and, between the two, in July of 1648, also have written the sort of *verse* found in the Elegy upon Villiers. Moreover, the fact that the Elegy's final lines (beginning, 'And we hereafter to his honour will / Not write so many, but so many kill') seem to imply that their author was fighting with the royalist forces makes most improbable their attribution to a notorious non-participant in the war.

5. Cambridge, 1968.

6. I am not convinced by George deF. Lord's arguments for attributing to Marvell the Second and Third Advices. See Lord's claims and Ephim G. Fogel's objections in *Bulletin of the New York Public Library*, LXII (1958), 551-70, and LXIII (1959), 223-36, 292-308, 355-66. The essays are reprinted in *Evidence for Authorship: Essays on Problems of Attribution*, ed. David V. Erdman and Ephim G. Fogel (Ithaca, N.Y., 1966). Lord prints the poems as Marvell's in his editions of *Poems on Affairs of State*, Vol. I: *1660-1678* (New Haven and London, 1963), and in *Andrew Marvell: Complete Poetry* (New York, 1968).

7. In 'The "Poetic Picture, Painted Poetry" of *The Last Instructions to a Painter*,' '*Modern Philology*,' LXIII (1966), 288-294, Earl Miner has explored the ways Marvell uses the conventions of the Painter poems to give unity.

8. Among other things, May had given a fulsome description of Charles as 'A King in Virtue and in Royalty' in 1633, just twelve years before he had written an introduction to *The King's Cabinet Opened*, a publication of the letters taken from the King at Naseby which included the canting remark: 'the drawing of this curtain may be as fatal to poetry, and all antichristian heresy here now, as the

rending of the veil was to the Jewish ceremonies in Judea at the expiration of our Saviour' (see A. G. Chester, *Thomas May: Man of Letters* [Philadelphia, 1932], pp. 167, 174). Among all the other charges I know of none to the effect that May was personally concerned about religion.

INDEX

Alabaster, William, 77
Ambrose, St., 151
Anacreon, 52
Andrewes, Lancelot, 87
Anne of Denmark, Queen, 87
Anne, Princess (Charles I's daughter), 177
Aquinas, St. Thomas, 137
Aubrey, John, 78, 119
Ausonius, 108

Bacon, Francis, 87
Baudelaire, Charles, 14, 129
Beaumont, Francis, 21, 52
Beaumont, Joseph, 102
Bedford, Lucy Russell, Countess of, 32, 77
Berthoff, Ann E., 188
Bishop, Elizabeth, 111
Blake, Robert, 164, 176
Blake, William, 114, 137
Blanshard, Rufus, A., 184
Boethius, 117
Bonaventura, St., 137
Brébeuf, Georges de, 133
Bridgeman, Orlando, 162
Brome, Richard, 67
Brooks, Cleanth, 184

Browning, Robert, 13
Bruno, Giordano, 74, 75
Buckingham, George Villiers, Duke of, 52
Buddha, 137
Burns, Robert, 14
Burton, Robert, 52
Bush, Douglas, 14-15, 40, 77, 80, 106, 112, 183
Buxton, John, 15, 183
Byron, George Gordon, Lord, 136

Cabillau, Baudouin, of Ypres, 105
Camden, William, 77
Carew, Thomas, *62-75*, 76, 78-79, 89, 102, 113, 132 178, 184; *Coelum Britannicum*, 74-75; Elegy on Donne, 64-66; Elegy on Maria Wentworth, 70; To Aurelian Townshend, 72-73; To Ben Jonson, 66-68; To George Sandys, 73-74; 'To my friend G. N., from Wrest,' 71-72
Carlisle, Lucy, Countess of, 63

191

117, 120, 122, 126, 131,
132, 159, 160, 162, 176,
178, 181, 183, 184; 'A
Celebration of Charis,'
27, 29, 44-45; Celia
poems, 27-28; *Epigrams*,
18-22; 'The faery beam
upon you,' 54; 'Hymn
to God the Father,' 30;
masques, 22, 29; 'My
Picture Left in Scotland,'
27; Ode on Cary and
Morison, 37-39; 'Still
to be neat,' 55-56;
Timber, 34; 'To Pens-
hurst,' 33-34; 'Why I
write not of Love,' 26
Juvenal, 23, 116

Keast, William R., 186
Keats, John, 137
Kermode, Frank, 138,
186-187, 188
King, Anne, 85-86
King, Henry, *76-86*, 88,
102, 184; 'Elegy upon
the most Incomparable
King Charles the First,'
82; 'The Exequy,' 84-
85; 'Sic Vita,' 83; 'To my
Sister Anne King, 85-86
King, John (father of
Henry), 76

King, John (brother of
Henry), 81
Koppel, Gene, 183
Koretz, Gene, 185

Lamb, Charles, 135
Laud, William, 76, 88
Lawes, Henry, 52
Lawes, William, 188
Legouis, Pierre, 186
Leishman, J. B., 131, 138
Leone Ebreo (Judah Leon
Abravanel), 137
Leopardi, Giacomo, 14
Lisle, George, 81
Locke, Matthew, 188
Lord, George de F., 186,
189
Lovelace, Richard, 48-49,
131, 164, 189
Lucas, Charles, 81
Lucretius, 13

McQueen, William A.,
187
Malraux, André, 161
Malvezzi, Virgilio, 118
Margoliouth, H. M., 188,
189
Marino, Giambattista, 69,
105, 108, 129
Marlowe, Christopher, 57
Martial, 52